INTERMARRIAGE AND JEWISH LIFE

INTER-MARRIAGE AND JEWISH LIFE

A Symposium

Edited by

Werner J. Cahnman

THE HERZL PRESS
and the
JEWISH RECONSTRUCTIONIST
PRESS   **NEW YORK**

97140

CONTENTS

*This book is dedicated to
my nephews and nieces
and
all their friends and agemates*

PREFACE

This book, containing the proceedings of the Conference on Intermarriage and Jewish Life, is the work of many people. The participants and authors deserve high praise for the selflessness of their cooperation; none of them received remuneration or expects royalties. In addition to the papers, each author prepared notes which, taken together and somewhat complemented as they are, by the editor, go a long way towards presenting a fairly complete bibliography on the topic of intermarriage, as it has its bearing on the Jewish community. Beyond the circle of the contributors, my appreciation goes first and foremost to Dr. Emil Lehmann, Director of the Theodor Herzl Institute, who facilitated the Conference in every way possible, suggested that the proceedings be published, and supported all further efforts with unfailing enthusiasm. Sincere thanks also go to Dr. Emanuel Neumann, President of the Theodor Herzl Foundation, who authorized the publication, Rabbi Ira Eisenstein, Director of the Reconstructionist Foundation, who secured the cooperation of the Reconstructionist Press, and Dr. Raphael Patai, Director of Research of the Theodor Herzl Institute, who helped with all the technicalities of the process and saw the book through the press. Finally, I should like to mention my colleague, Prof. Joseph Maier, and my wife, Dr. Gisella L. Cahnman, without whose constant encouragement and active assistance the work could not have been completed.

The Editor

7

INTRODUCTION
by
Werner J. Cahnman

I

When I was a boy of twelve years of age, I took from my father's bookshelf a copy of Arthur Ruppin's *"Die Juden der Gegenwart"* ("The Jews of Today") and read it avidly. My family were amazed that I took so much interest in the dry stuff of demography, but it is not very hard to understand why Ruppin's argument aroused me greatly and made me conscious of what was then called the "Jewish question." Ruppin demonstrated that the post-emancipatory Jew had deprived himself of the shelter of religious law; that he had become secularized and urbanized; and that with secularization and urbanization had come smaller families, conversion, indifference and intermarriage. He further showed that the children from Jewish-Christian intermarriages, in most instances, were lost to Judaism. Ruppin concluded that the alternative posed by this development which, he thought, could not be reversed, was clear: either assimilation to the point of dissolution in the diaspora or concentration and survival in a Jewish homeland in Palestine.

Such was the Zionist position of those days. The creation of the State of Israel, which we have witnessed in this generation, has changed the situation insofar as, with the center assured, the existence of the periphery began to assume a new importance. To the problem of bracing up the diaspora by means of a Jewish State was now added the problem of securing the continued existence of the State of Israel by means of a vigorous Jewish settlement in other countries. Also, it was recognized that the new diaspora in America, in many regards, was different from the old one in Europe. Everything is more complex and fluid here, full of danger, to be sure, but also rich with promise. Hence, Zionism necessarily has acquired a concern with Jewish survival in the diaspora, not as an alternative to the State of Israel, but as an indispensable complement to it. In these circumstances, to cope with intermarriage where one finds it becomes a foremost concern.

At the same time, intermarriage is very much of an American problem. Historically speaking, America is empty space filled with teeming humanity. From the earliest days people from everywhere arrived in this country, mingled and produced offspring, but the process has never been completed. Obstacles arose which checked it effectively. Earlier waves of immigration, chiefly Anglo-Saxon in origin, have established themselves on top of the stratification pyramid and have assimilated to their status position individuals from other groups, but not entire groups as such. As a result, other groups, among whom the Irish and the Jews are most conspicuous, have established secondary status hierarchies. Another result of the acculturation of growing numbers of minority members to the Anglo-Saxon mode of life, thought and speech was that the fortress of Anglo-Saxon social privilege could be protected only by means of discriminatory practices, some rude, as in the case of the Negroes, and some subtle, as in the case of varied immigrant groups, especially the Jews. Hence, minority members were thrown upon their own resources and forces working against intermarriage emerged nearly as potent as those working for it. It is perhaps not incorrect to say that intermarriage proceeds, but that the process tends to be slowed down considerably. At any rate, from a general as well as from a Jewish point of view, the study of intermarriage must be considered crucial for the understanding of intergroup relations.

II.

All these, and similar, deliberations lay at the bottom of the "Conference on Intermarriage and Jewish Life," which was convened by the Theodor Herzl Institute in New York on February 13 and 14, 1960. In order to appreciate what the conveners had in mind, a few words must be said about the organizational idea of the present book of proceedings and about the contributors.

There could have been no thought of gathering definitive data either about the scope of intermarriage between Jews and non-Jews in this country or about the motivations leading to such unions; nor was it intended to suggest a course of action. Most of the available data are of dubious validity and hardly representative or capable of generalization. But this does not do away with the fact that the interested public clamors for information and for guidance, no matter how incomplete the information and how tentative the guidance. Somehow, the scattered data had to be assembled and evaluated. Where no data were available, we attempted at least to outline the problems and to suggest approaches. From the point of view of the scholar in the social sciences the outcome is far from perfect, but it is hoped that the service rendered will be considered useful in the circumstances.

The idea of the conference was to bring together rabbis and Jewish educators, on the one hand, and social scientists, on the other. These two groups are very different in their professional outlook. The rabbi and educator is the guardian of the heritage, while the social scientist is an objective observer. Of course, both concerns, although essentially contradictory, may be present in one and the same person. For instance, Rabbi Eichhorn's and Rabbi Cohen's contributions, the fact that they represent a definite point of view notwithstanding, qualify as documents of objective scholarship, while Louis Rosenberg's contribution does not conceal concern about the heritage. My own contribution serves the purpose of combining concern with the Jewish heritage and with the maintenance of democratic processes in America, and to hold up both of these concerns against the data of objective research. Prof. Kennedy's contribution surely shows concern with trends in American society, couched, however, in the tentative language of scholarship. Rabbi Rubenstein, as a student of psychoanalysis, shows concern with the happiness of the individual, but this concern is not absent from other contributions. Each one of the contributors has his personal equation, but all strive to understand undisguised reality. The result is a far-reaching convergence. The approaches differ, but the conclusions point in the same direction. This is perhaps as good a test of reliability as any.

Differences are somewhat more pronounced in the mode of presentation. The spoken word addresses itself to the mood of the hour while the printed page aims at leaving a lasting impact. Some contributors, like Rabbi Weisberger, prefer to let the spoken word stand, in an effort to preserve the momentary impulse; others, like Prof. Maier, like to objectify. Some, like Rabbi Eichhorn and Prof. Kennedy, read from a prepared manuscript which they had to change but little afterwards, while others, like Prof. Ben-Horin and myself, set themselves the task of translating the oratorical phrase into the more detached language of the essay. Some, like Prof. Rosenthal, contracted in writing what they had said at the Conference; others, like Rabbi Rubenstein, elaborated. However, Rabbi Cohen, L. Rosenberg, Jacob Baar Alvin Chenkin and Jacob Zukerman, who were not present at the Conference, had no such problem.

The outline has a certain symphonic quality. It opens with the double *"leitmotif"* of Jewish concern and sociological appraisal. The core of the data presentation is contained in Part II, but some specific areas of application are elaborated in Part III. The double *"leitmotif"* reappears in the concluding part, with roles reversed: Jewish concern now has the last word. Regarding the sociological appraisal, the emphasis is shifted somewhat in that Prof. Kennedy presents the viewpoint of social science pure and simple while my own piece is more complex inasmuch as it attempts to submit the fullness of the intervening discussion to sociological conceptualization.

A few words must be said about technical matters, chiefly referring to terminology. Commonly, the term intermarriage is used for a wide variety of phenomena. It covers the marriage between spouses of different racial, ethnic and religious origin and a combination of these; only the marriage between spouses of different social status, although it lurks ominously behind the other differentiations, is not covered. Such inter-class marriages are called *"mèsalliance"* from the point of view of the upper status group and "a stroke of luck" from the point of view of the lower status group. We cannot follow up on this alluring aspect any further. In the present context, intermarriage is generally understood to mean marriage between spouses of different religious identification; if one spouse is converted to the religion of the other prior to the marriage, no intermarriage in this sense occurs. This differs from the usage of some authors who extend the term intermarriage to include all legitimate mixtures of strains, including those involving conversion; the term mixed marriage is then introduced to designate marriage of spouses of different religion. Needless to say that mixed marriage, or intermarriage in a narrower sense, as used in this book, is the truly novel phenomenon in a secularized society. Intermarriage in a wider sense is universal.

To subsume Jewish-Gentile marriages under the religious label is not to deny the ethnic quality of being Jewish, merely to say that such quality is evidenced in our society in religious preference. Much confusion could be avoided if the terms used were always made unmistakably clear. For instance, Prof. Toynbee, in his recent advocacy of "intermarriage" between Jews and Christians, may have had in mind either intermarriage with both spouses remaining religiously separate, but mutually tolerant, or intermarriage with one spouse converting to Christianity, or intermarriage with one spouse converting to Judaism. From the point of view of all the contributors to the present volume, the latter alternative is entirely acceptable; from the point of view of the majority, preferable. One would have liked to know what Prof. Toynbee prefers.

The individual contributions are speaking for themselves, but clarifying remarks here and there may be in order. I consider Prof. Kennedy's paper especially valuable because it holds up the mirror of the "generalized other" to the otherwise dangerously isolated Jewish "self." I wish to add some comment, however. Prof. Kennedy considers the Jewish dietary laws as constituting a wall of separation between Jews and Gentiles. As far as social intercourse is concerned, this is correct, but not regarding intermarriage, if and when the non-Jewish spouse, in converting to Judaism, accepts the dietary laws along with the other obligations of Jewish ritual behavior. Of course, this is intermarriage only in the wider sense of the term, not in the narrower sense in which it is employed in this symposium. Moreover, at the present moment and in the foreseeable future, the foregoing applies only to a minority of American Jews. For the majority, the dietary laws are either observed in the home, but not abroad, or completely disregarded. In all these instances, the opportunities for intermingling are legion. If the opportunity is not grasped, the obstacle may be—more often than not—the reluctance of the Gentile rather than the unwillingness of the Jew. The second comment concerns ethnicity. While it is true that religion and ethnicity are inseparable in Jewish existence, this view tends to obscure the fact that Jewish immigration to America has been culturally as diversified as any other immigration and that these ethno-cultural strains have intermingled as much as comparable strains have among Protestants and Catholics. Genealogical and statistical studies will have to delineate this process some time in the future.

The third comment referring to Prof. Kennedy's paper is about intermarriage rates. Prof. Kennedy considers them to be low and to constitute a brake on assimilation. Her view has recently been supported by C. Bezalel Sherman in his book, *The Jew within American Society* (Detroit, 1960), wherein he demonstrates that the rate of Jewish-Gentile intermarriage is lower in the United States than in all other countries from which comparable data are available and that the rate of increase is exceptionally low also. However, this conclusion is open to challenge, if it is used as a basis for prediction. As Prof. Rosenthal in his paper, "Acculturation without Assimilation?" (*Am. Journal of Sociology*, vol. LXVI, No. 3, Nov. 1960, pp. 275-

289), points out, two lines of argument are possible. To quote Rosenthal:

> "If we accept the findings of the 1957 survey of the United States Bureau of the Census of a national inter-marriage rate [for Jews] of 7.2% and if, at the same time, we assume that the statistics for Iowa and the San Francisco area [31%, 17.2%, 20% and 37%, respectively] are merely regional variations of the over-all rate, we can probably be justified in defending the current survival formula as adequate for the preservation of the Jewish group. If we assume, however, that the findings for Iowa and San Francisco are the first indications of the future over-all rate of intermarriage, then the efficacy of the survival formula must be seriously doubted."

The second line of approach is strengthened by the fact that the Bureau of the Census considers the recorded percentage of mixed couples as a minimum figure. The same assumption applies to private studies, such as the ones recently undertaken in Washington, D.C., San Francisco and elsewhere. The reason is that interviewers can ascertain only those cases of intermarriage where the different religion of spouses is openly declared. Furthermore, cases of conversion are not subsumed under "intermarriage" and consequently are not covered in interview schedules. It is therefore my considered opinion that the available statistical data are insufficient for the appreciation of the amount of intermarriage and intermixture between Jews and non-Jews in the United States. They are minimal figures only.

Challenging as Prof. Kennedy's paper is, the subsequent papers are no less important. Prof. Ben Horin's thoughtful piece, calling for the strengthening of the "little Zions" of the heart and for the Jewish dedication of the family corresponds to Rabbi Cohen's admonition that Jews must look to the quality of their family relationships, their communal enterprises, their cultural concerns. L. Rosenberg points to the same thing, when he speaks about a deeper knowledge or a deterrent to intermarriage. Prof. Rosenthal adds a question mark in this regard while my own contribution speaks of education for a unified world. Rabbi Cohen's further admonition that intermarriage ought to be considered a "leaven" rather than a danger, is echoed in practically all the papers in this volume. The similarity of opinion and conclusion in this respect is noteworthy. It shows that a democratic Judaism in Mordecai M. Kaplan's sense is emerging in the invigorating American environment. (Prof. Kaplan's classic passage from *Judaism as a Civilization* is quoted in my contribution to this volume.) Rabbi Eichhorn was asked specifically to draw attention to the relation between intermarriage and conversion, but the theme re-occurs, although unsolicited, in psycho-analytical garb in Rabbi Rubenstein's contribution; it shows up in the concluding sentence of Rabbi Weisberger's piece; it forms a major strand in my own paper; it is found elsewhere. The reader is asked to do his own thinking along this line.

The papers by Baar, Rosenberg, Rosenthal and Maier carry the burden of documentation. Louis Rosenberg and Baar-Cahnman take advantage of the fact that census forms as well as vital statistics in Switzerland and Canada have reference to religion and hence yield data which are not found in the Census of the United States. Also, processes of acculturation seem further progressed in Switzerland than in the United States, so that data from there, if used with caution, may be of predictive value. Intermarriage data from Canada, where acculturative processes have barely begun to operate, are revealing with this aspect in mind. The Canadian figures support my previous contention that the available American data on intermarriage are incomplete.

The very conciseness of Prof. Rosenthal's paper is significant. It shows what we actually know about intermarriage between Jews and non-Jews in the U.S.A. and how very scanty that knowledge is. Consequently, Prof. Maier's paper must be considered an indispensable link in the total argument of this volume. What we don't know, or barely know, looms too large to be overlooked. I venture to predict that Prof. Maier's survey of "unresearched problems" will be used widely. His review of the literature reveals many desperate stabs in the dark and raises many challenging questions, but it cannot provide the answers. In a way, Rabbi Weisberger's and Rabbi Trainin's pieces are a pathetic confirmation of this dearth of answers. Rabbi Weisberger's paper offers an impressionistic picture of the problems which arise from contact situations in small communities, especially in the South. Rabbi Trainin's brief remarks are preceded by an outline of the problems with which the researcher in metropolitan areas is confronted. This outline, drawn by a statistician and a social worker who are both conversant with the situation, shows the magnitude of the task which lies ahead. Rabbi Trainin, Mr. Zukerman and Mr. Chenkin, from their vantage point within the Federation of Jewish Philanthropies of New York, join Prof. Maier in a call to scholarly foundations and communal institutions to provide the means for the many kinds of studies that are needed, if one wants to assay the scope of intermarriage, to understand the phenomenon of intermarriage, and to provide intelligent guidance in the field of intermarriage. The editor expresses the faint hope that the call may not go entirely unheeded.

TWOFOLD GUIDANCE

WHAT HAS SOCIAL SCIENCE TO SAY
ABOUT INTERMARRIAGE?

By Ruby Jo Reeves Kennedy

Social scientists study society and the social behavior of man. The structure and organization of society is one important area of concentration. We know that man has survived by living in groups with others like himself. Within the large group—called society—there have always been sub-divisions made up of people who grouped themselves together for many reasons. Our interest tonight is in these sub-divisions within the larger structure of society.

In particular, our attention is focused upon two questions: 1) why does a minority group continue to exist when assimilation into the dominant group is not only possible but even advantageous and desirable from many points of view? and 2) why do sub-groups remain distinctive and separate in some ways, but not in all ways?

Many explanations have been offered for the existence of sub-groups. William Graham Sumner attributed them to "ethnocentrism" which is a feeling of group superiority. Giddings spoke of a "consciousness of kind" which draws and holds people together. I think that man's search for "security" is still another reason that binds people together. This is a kind of "sociological" security which, as I see it, is a deliberate attempt on the part of a sub-group to remain a cohesive unit in order to attain and maintain a kind of emotional and intellectual integration and "safeness" which sets it apart from the majority group in important ideological and philosophical matters.

To do this, a sub-group would have to be in the highly advantageous position of being able to select ways in which it wished to integrate into the majority group and ways in which it preferred to remain apart. In other words, this kind of minority or sub-group operates on a selective basis and can do so only because of the particular internal strength which it possesses.

From my study and reading of the literature in the field and on the basis of my limited research, the Jews seem to be this kind of sub-group in American society today. Jews are recognized, they are spoken of, they are referred to as a sub-group sufficiently cohesive and integrated and different, to be identified as such. I must say, to begin with, I understand that there is not *one* Jewish group but, in fact, several with each recognizing differences between itself and the others. In an earlier period these groups, arriving at different times in America, were rather clearly delineated in several ways with a distinctive cultural heritage characterizing each, and with the main differences pertaining to religious ideas and practices.

Regardless of these internal differences the Jews seem to constitute a minority or sub-group sufficiently integrated within itself and sufficiently different from others to be recognized and identified as such. It is my further thought that this separateness will persist as long as the group observes certain behavior practices which tend to promote this kind of cohesiveness.

Cultural assimilation between differing groups is furthered by many factors, such as learning and speaking the dominant language; the adoption of clothing and food habits of the dominant group; the acceptance and participation in the educational system of the society; the active and full functioning in all economic pursuits of the society; and intermarrying freely on a non-discriminatory or non-preferential basis. By the latter I do not mean that marriage is non-selective on an individual, personal basis, but I mean that there are no preferential marriage groups as such. If these things I have mentioned are indices by which cultural assimilation may be measured, then all the facts with which I am familiar indicate rather conclusively that Jews are completely assimilated in all respects except one and that is the last index, namely, they do not intermarry freely but stress preference for endogamy or marriage within the group.

I hasten to add that the existence of preferential marriage-groups is not something new. Ethnology and anthropology yield much evidence that this has been customary among almost all peoples about which there is any information. Usually, however, with prolonged culture contact, accompanied by pervasive contact in a society, there is a lessening of endogamy and a weakening of the emotional and intellectual support of preferential marriage groups. This, I think, has occurred much more slowly among Jews in American society than has the participation of that group into all other facets of American life.

For instance, Jews are completely assimilated in use of English, the dominant language; in dressing similarly; in supporting actively the general educational system. At this point, I should say that we must not overlook the teaching of Hebrew to Jewish children but this is on the side, so to speak. Incidentally, this program is, in general, sanctioned, reinforced, and supported by the family and for the main purpose of becoming familiar with Jewish culture which can be done most effectively by a mastery of the principal language in which it is written. There is no thought of teaching Hebrew to children for everyday usage or even to be spoken as a second language. So, I view this as something rather special and do not envisage it as a factor either reducing or militating against assimilation. Actually, the understanding of Hebrew is essential to active participation in religious services. In addition, the teaching and learning of Hebrew is, in itself, a meritorious religious and intellectual activity.

With reference to food habits, in so far as I know, Jews constitute the only sizable minority group in America which retains some distinctive traditional food habits and practices. (The Chinese do, but they do not constitute, statistically, a group comparable in size with the Jews). I am not referring to the tabooing of certain foods on particular occasions. Neither am I referring to popular food habits introduced into our eating patterns by ethnic groups such as the Chinese, the Japanese, the Italians, the Greeks, the Spanish, and others. These foods represent, for the most part, special seasoning, combinations, even techniques of cooking which have gained considerable favor with the general eating public. What I have in mind with reference to Jewish food habits and practices is the actual preparation of food in a prescribed way, particularly the slaughtering of meat, as well as the manner in which "processed" foods must be done. These special food requirements seem to be sufficiently significant to the group for there to be maintained their own meat markets, which sell only meat slaughtered according to ritual procedures and for their processed foods to be ritually supervised and approved by the placing of a rabbinical "seal of approval" on the package.

I understand that these food habits and practices have a long history and that, in the opinion of some observers at least, most if not all of the original reasons for their observance no longer exist, yet the rules do, and that is what interests the social scientist who is studying assimilation. Why have these particular practices persisted to the extent that they have? There must be many reasons, most of which I do not know, for I am not a student of Jewish culture, but they seem to be related to marriage and the family and this is, as I mentioned earlier, the one facet of life in which I think Jews remain separate and, in this particular instance, at some inconvenience and certainly with economic overtones. By the continued insistence upon this special food habit, which must be practiced by and within the family, this means that a tight and powerful control operates in the selection of a marriage partner who will be sympathetic to this food habit and willing to participate in the observance of it. In connection with this, I was interested in the statement made by Maurice Fishberg who said that "as long as Jews adhere to their religious practices and rigidly observe the dietary laws, no marriage between them and other faiths can take place."[1] In general Fishberg is probably right, but certainly not in particular. By that I mean that mixed marriages do occur. This is a statistical fact. I would agree that this distinctive food practice has probably been one important factor in limiting intermarriage, but not in eliminating it.

In his recent book, *This is My God,* Mr. Wouk stresses the importance of food and of eating. He says that people forget many things but that eating is not one of them, and comments upon the amount of time and effort that is devoted to eating. He points out that in the United States the observance of Jewish food laws is now increasing after what had appeared a generation ago to be a diminution of this practice, and concludes his discussion of the significance of this in this way, "food laws are social instruments for keeping the Jewish nation alive and psychologi-

cal instruments for preserving the identity of individuals."[2] I understand that some authorities feel the Jewish
dietary practices are either disappearing altogether or being altered rather drastically, but Mr. Wouk does not seem
to be of this opinion.

Available facts indicate that Jews are engaged in all
kinds of jobs and occupations and at all income levels. In
other words, Jews do not appear to concentrate in or dom-
inate any job or occupation. It is true that the proportions
they constitute of the several occupations differ from the
proportions that the general population constitute of the
same occupations. For instance, there are far more Jews
than non-Jews in the professional, managerial and official
class, in clerical and skilled occupations, whereas there are
far fewer Jews than non-Jews in semi-skilled and un-
skilled occupations.

I feel sure that this occupational disparity is a clear reflection on the part of Jews of an emphasis upon learning
and training with a long history of their being urban, rather than rural dwellers and of their being non-manual workers. Zborowski says that "In blending the American success pattern with the *shtetl* emphasis upon book learning,
something of the early veneration of learning appears to
have remained. It is not merely that to work with the head
carries more status than to work with the hands. There is
also a feeling that intellectual activity is better than manual activity in the sense of being more enjoyable and also
of being morally superior."[3] He also points out that even
though social significance may predominate over religious
significance among highly acculturated Jews in the United
States, the idea of being learned carries much prestige,
status and pecuniary gain. Even Jews in lower occupations
are said to have a greater respect for learning than is usual
among manual or low-paid workers elsewhere.

We have here in the Jewish group, then, a group admiration for learning, a long history of devotion to it, and, furthermore, a kind of responsibility which the Jewish family has characteristically been expected to discharge with reference to training for learning.

I am reminded at this point of Simon Rabinsky and his two sons Jakov and Jossi in *Exodus,* and the stirring account of life in the 'Pale' in Russia where the daily existence of poverty, discrimination and deprivation was enriched by constant devotion and assiduous application to religious studies which "contained information on everything from social behavior to personal cleanliness." Simon Rabinsky sought—and succeeded in—instilling in his sons the joy and delight of the "conquest of the mind" for, as the author said "In the Pale where nearly everyone was destitute the measure of a man's wealth was his knowledge."[4]

In his analysis of this aspect of Jewish life, Zborowski also points out that the emphasis upon learning which is so strong in the life of traditional Jews has actually diminished but little in intensity on different levels of acculturation in America although, as he says, the objective of learning and the fields of learning have changed, the keen striving toward intellectual activity has persisted.

This, as a part of Jewish family life, was again demonstrated and under quite different circumstances in Fauman's Detroit study of Jewish and non-Jewish sons. In his discussion of the occupational differences within the Jewish group itself, I found especially provocative his conclusions that "theoretically, the differences between Jews themselves in occupational adjustment are greatest where (1) attachment to traditional Jewish life is greatest" and (2) "the length of stay in America is the least."[5]

These ideas are related to our present discussion in two ways: (1) the strength of family influence is postively related to the observance within the family of traditional

Jewish values; and (2) Jewish family life is weakened with assimilation, that is, a blending into the dominant or majority groups, as one continues to live with that group and to identify increasingly with its values and practices. In his recent book, *Jews in Suburbia,* Gordon referred to this in still another way when he said that "parents are concerned with the fact that . . . . living in a predominantly non-Jewish environment will be accompanied by increasing intermarriage" and for that reason frequently said to him, "we want to get our children into communities where they will meet more Jewish boys and girls."[6]

This brings me to my main thesis—namely, it seems to me that it is in affairs dealing with the family that the Jews demonstrate a marked degree of cohesiveness as a sub-group in American society. And—I go on to add—this continued separateness seems to be the consequence of effort on the part of the group to maintain its distinctive internal integration. This would, obviously, begin with marriage and with the crucial questions of (1) who marries whom, and (2) whether the selection of a marriage partner is an entirely personal, individual matter resting with each boy and girl or whether the group has given some attention to this and has established preferential rules; and (3) how much effort does the group exercise in having these preferential rules observed. These questions are for our consideration. I shall make no special effort to answer them directly because I cannot do so in any documented, scientific way.

It is generally accepted that the family is the foundation stone, so to speak, of society. A frequently reiterated platitude is that a strong, stable society reflects strong, stable families. Another popular and probably very sound opinion is that a strong individual personality is more than likely the consequence of a strong, unified family life. Much has been said with reference to predicting happiness and success in marriage on the basis of happy and maritally successful parents. All of these things seem to point to a matching of marriage partners. On the basis of their studies, some social scientists predict that people with similar interests, similar educations, similar religions, similar social and economic backgrounds in general are much more likely to make a success of their marriages than persons dissimilar in these respects.

Various authorities have noted that Jews place much emphasis upon a strong, unified family pattern which is reinforced and supported by various cultural ceremonials concerning the crisis periods of life (birth, the advent of puberty, marriage, burial) as well as upon certain daily procedures and practices of a dietary nature. Obviously, the more similar are the interests and backgrounds of people, the easier is it to maintain a strong, unified family system with the tensions and dissensions then coming mainly from outside the family rather than from within it. This is true in general, but particularly so when the subgroup has beliefs, rules, rituals, and practices unique to it, and also when the family unit is charged, so to speak, within the pattern of daily living with seeing to it that these rules, rituals, and practices are observed. It is far easier and more likely that these things will be done when both parties have the same interests and the same religious background than when they have not.

Some social scientists have felt that increased secularization and the lessened control of the church over its members has been accompanied by changes in the family's attitude toward marriage and the selection of marriage partners in particular. It is predicted that intermarriage will increase as the daily practice of certain cultural and religious rituals ceases being a fundamental part of the pattern of Jewish family life and that, I am sure, is what the parents had in mind when they were talking with Mr.

Gordon. Several social scientists, for instance Bossard, have noted that marriages between Jews and Gentiles have actually increased with the decline of the observance of daily rituals among the Jews. Of course in order to determine just how decisive a factor this is as far as influencing the rate of intermarriage is concerned, we would need many more case studies of such marriages than are available now.

At this point I wish to mention the work of Milton Barron, who in his book, *"People Who Intermarry"*, reports that from the latter part of the 19th century until the advent of Hitler, Jewish-Gentile intermarriage increased throughout Europe. He goes on to conclude that Jewish intermarriage proceeds at a higher rate during periods when discrimination is lowest and anti-semitic feelings are low. This is a very provocative thought which I would like to see carefully documented by statistical research.

Some early research in this country revealed that nativity was an important factor in determining the extent of intermarriage with there being a high incidence of endogamy not only on an ethnic basis but also on a nativity basis. That is, foreign-born were much more likely to marry foreign-born than native-born. Several studies revealed that while this was true of practically all ethnic groups, it was more so of some than others. Obviously, with the decrease of immigration, there is less intermarriage of this kind. Pertinent, however, to our discussion is one conclusion arrived at by Prof. Bossard in observing differences in the intermarriage rates of various ethnic groups. He found the lowest intermarriage rates, regardless of nativity, among the Russians about whom he said the situation was affected by the fact that many of them were of Jewish descent. He pointed out quite definitely in his study of the native-born and foreign-born in New York State that of all groups, the Jews practiced the highest degree of endogamy.

Now, very briefly, for a few facts about the degree or extent of intermarriage. In New York City, between 1908 and 1912 only 2 per cent of the Jews who married, married out. In Cincinnati between 1916 and 1919, only 3.6 per cent of the Jews who married, married out. In Stamford, Connecticut in 1938, only 7.2 per cent of all the Jewish marriages functioning at that time were intermarriages.[7] In Burlington, Vermont—where no statistics were shown—Ellen Anderson commented that the Jews had the lowest intermarriage rate of all groups.[8] In a recent study in Iowa, Chancellor and Monahan showed a fairly high degree of intermarriage, but felt there were too few cases upon which to generalize.[9] A recent survey in Washington indicated that approximately 12 per cent of the households in that area were mixed marriages. A study in the Los Angeles area in 1958 revealed that 7 per cent of the Jews had married gentiles (incidentally, this statistic had not changed significantly since 1951). Gordon also says that "the rate of intermarriage tended to increase among the native-born children of native-born parents reaching a proportion of about 7.4 per cent of the population", and he goes on to comment that this "accentuates the fact that intermarriage will increase whenever and wherever Jews live in communities that are not exclusively Jewish."[10]

With reference to my own research in New Haven, these are my findings for the Jewish group:

1870	100	per cent married in;
1900	98.8	per cent married in;
1930	97.0	per cent married in;
1940	93.7	per cent married in;
1950	94.9	per cent married in;
1955	97.4	per cent married in.[10a]

Gordon reports that a recent study in greater Washington revealed that 12 per cent of the households in that area were mixed marriages, with the proportion being even higher in suburban Prince George County (20.8 per cent) and higher still in some suburbs immediately adjacent to Washington (34 per cent). He then goes on to conclude: "Given a continuation of 'good times' and freedom from open anti-Semitism, we may expect the average rate of intermarriage for the nation to reach 10 per cent within the decade."[10b]

The rate or extent of intermarriage of Jews with non-Jews seems to be related to the size of the community, as well as to the size of the Jewish group within the community. This, of course, has to do with the number of available mates at hand. Jews have traditionally been and still are urban dwellers, so one might reasonably expect endogamy to be higher in cities where the Jewish group is likely to be large enough to have at all times an available supply of marriageable people of both sexes than in small or even middle-sized communities where the Jewish subgroup might not be very large. I regret that I cannot cite conclusive statistics to prove this point but several researchers have arrived at this conclusion. In New Haven where I have done my research, I have found this to be true, but that is a community in which the Jewish group is believed to be sufficiently large for there to be available partners of both sexes. In Iowa, on the other hand, where the intermarriage rate was high, the authors pointed out that the Jewish population constituted less than 1 per cent of the total population and I feel sure that their unwillingness to generalize was due to the paucity of available Jewish marriage partners in that part of the country.

With reference to Rabbi Gordon's conclusion, it is my thought that intermarriage is increasing. I have shown this in my New Haven material, but I think the important point is not that it is increasing, but the very slight extent to which it has increased and his prediction that within the next decade the increase may be as much as 10 per cent. This would mean, then, that 90 per cent of all Jewish marriages would be with Jews and that, to me, indicates an amazingly high degree of endogamy—more so than is attained by any other white minority group in America. Furthermore, even if the intermarriage rate were to increase to 20 or 25 or even 30 per cent—this would still mean that 80 or 75 or 70 per cent of all Jewish marriages were in-marriages—and this also would, I feel sure, still be the highest degree of endogamy reached by any other white minority group.

As you can see, I have not attempted to explain why Jews marry Jews or why Jews marry Gentiles; nor have I attempted to delineate or describe those who do either of these things. Several social scientists have concerned themselves with these aspects of the problem and have presented some ideas as to the types of persons doing each of these things. Interesting as are the conclusions drawn by these researchers, I am inclined to doubt that the types, or any types for that matter, would pertain exclusively to Jews. The same or certainly quite similar types might well be delineated in any sub-group which had traditionally practiced endogamy, but was now faced with the task of assimilation into a new and different dominant or, at any rate, general culture.

In connection with this, I wish to say that in cases of mixed marriage, several alternatives are possible. Both persons may leave their respective faiths, or each spouse may continue to practice his or her own particular faith, or there may be a conversion of one spouse to the faith of the other. In the event of the last, there is, of course, the possibility that the Gentile may be converted to the Jewish faith and this, I understand, is happening more often now than formerly. I can not document this at all, but I mention it to suggest that intermarriage does not inevitably and automatically mean with this—or any group—the loss of adherents. It might, on the other hand, mean a gain of adherents.

I now wish to refer to the Bossard-Boll researches on marriage and in particular to their study entitled *One Marriage-Two Faiths*. In this they report a steady increase of intermarriage for all spouses, and give considerable attention to the consequences of mixed marriages and various kinds of adjustments to such unions. They conclude that, to be successful and happy, all marriages must be worked at diligently, for a "good" family is an achievement, not an accident and seldom ever happens automatically. In the event of religious intermarriage, the difficulties may be greater, the obstacles more numerous, but such marriages can and do succeed when worked at cooperatively, consciously, sensibly and intelligently by all members of the family.[11] Jewish intermarriages were among the cases studied and analyzed by these two social scientists.

My interest is in another aspect, namely, that exogamy (or intermarriage) by whomever and for whatever reason is usually regarded by social scientists as indicating a lessening or dimunition of the cohesiveness of a sub-group and that if this pattern increases and continues it would surely ultimately mean free and uncontrolled marriage. If and when the latter happens, then I would say that complete and thorough-going assimilation has occurred, for surely the most decisive factor of the full acceptance of one person by another, or of one group by another, is marriage.

Returning now to my main point: Jewish intermarriage is increasing but much more slowly, proportionately, than in any other white minority group. There is not one ethnic or religious group which is, of course, quite comparable with the Jews as far as endogamy is concerned. This I pointed out for six different intervals in New Haven between 1870 and 1955. I am well aware of the fact that New Haven must not be regarded as representative or typical of the entire country, but the other studies—few in number—still reveal that Jews practice a higher rate of endogamy than any other ethnic or religious group.

Our larger interest is in the area of assimilation and, for me, an inspection of intermarriage is done for the sole purpose of determining, in so far as this is possible, what has been the trend in this regard. As I stated earlier, it is my feeling that endogamy in modern America reflects the deliberate desire of a sub-group—if white—to remain apart for emotional and philosophical reasons which are usually related to an integrated family system.

I wish to mention a few things which may be interpreted as reflecting a strong, unified, integrated pattern of family life among any group, but I shall now use the Jewish group to illustrate. I hasten to say that although sociologists stress the relationship of family solidarity to such things as delinquency and alcoholism, they recognize that a high or low incidence of these must not be attributed to any particular kind of family life or, for that matter, to any particular kind of religion. This is because the total configuration (the home, the neighborhood, nativity, education, economic status, religion, and race) is important. We know that it is impossible in our complex society to isolate any one factor as causing delinquency, alcoholism and so on. Nevertheless, we do feel that the family is one of the several important influences which bear directly upon the individual and contribute to a very considerable extent to the development of his personality.

I shall now speak briefly about delinquency and alcoholism, but I must again caution you against thinking that I am saying that with pronounced endogamy comes inevitably and automatically a strong, cohesive family, out of which there come few delinquents and alcoholics. This is not what I am saying, but I do say that the low incidence of these particular behavior problems among Jews merits consideration. And this is coupled with the further fact that Jews certainly do have the highest in-marriage rate of any white minority group.

Investigations in Europe and America have revealed low adult and juvenile crime rates among Jews. I can't develop this topic, but I wish to refer to the research of Sophia Robison in New York City and to her general conclusion that the rate of juvenile delinquency among Jews is very low. She says that if Jewish children were delinquent in correct proportions to population size there should have been almost ten times as many Jewish delinquents as there were in actual fact. She goes on to say that "it is doubtful whether any religious group in New York City can rival the Jews as regards infrequency of delinquency", but adds "despite this, the fear has been expressed that the Jewish youth of today are far less law-abiding than those of a generation or two ago."[12]

The Yale Center of Alcoholic Studies reports that research here and abroad has shown that the rate of alcoholism and other drinking pathologies among Jews is very low, and that this is so despite the fact that the drinking of alcoholic beverages has been widespread among the Jews since ancient times. The Yale researchers attribute the rarity of Jewish alcoholism to social and cultural traditions[13] for which there is reinforcement in the Old Testament and in subsequent rabbinical writings in the form of denunciations of drunkenness even though "they did hold alcohol in good esteem and at times even prescribed it. 'Give strong drink unto him that is ready to perish,' the Book of Proverbs proclaims, and 'wine unto those that be of heavy hearts. Let him drink, and forget his poverty, and remember his misery no more.'"[14]

In his recent book, Vance Packard discusses the aversion

of Jews to alcoholism and attributes this to two causes, namely, (1) the Jews' tremendous respect for intellectual accomplishment coupled with the feeling that "drunkenness undermines—at least for a time—one's intellectual capacity" and (2) to the fact that "Jews see alcohol as a threat to self-control. Historically, Jews, as a persecuted group, have had to be alert constantly to threats to their family and their life."[15]

In Snyder's study on alcoholism he points out that "the assimilating Jews who have increasing contacts with Gentiles are more prone to drunkenness and alcoholism than their compatriots of the ghetto."[16] And on this same point Mr. Packard notes, "the younger Jew, if he lives in a Gentile area, will serve martinis to his guests before dinner, and may even, to be congenial, have a bar in his house. However, if he lives in a predominantly Jewish area, he drinks very sparingly; and if a Gentile visits his home he is, out of habit, more likely to offer food than drink as a refreshment."[15] All I can do here, of course, is to point to these correlations, not to draw any premature conclusions.

I wish to close my remarks, however, by mentioning one major conclusion or generalization expressed by the majority of social scientists who are students of marriage and the family, namely, that the selection of marriage partners in American society is generally homogamous. This means that people marry people similar to themselves as far as almost all social characteristics are concerned, but the most important seems to be religious similarity. Stated another way, most marriages are endogamous as far as religion is concerned. This has been demonstrated a good many times, and has been verified many more times by attitudinal studies. Both types of research have shown this to be generally characteristic of the three main religious groups—Catholics, Protestants, and Jews and, parenthetic-

ally, even within certain denominations within the Protestant group. But statistical research (which, after all, is
a record of what people actually do) has revealed quite
conclusively that the extent of Jewish in-marriage is the
highest of all religious groups.

I think that this high incidence of Jewish in-marriage
is because the Jewish religion—as does also the Catholic
Church and some of the Protestant denominations—stresses
endogamy. But the "stressing" is reinforced vigorously in
the Jewish group by a particularly cohesive, ritualistically
patterned type of family life which can continue to exist
most safely by sanctioning, furthering, and promoting
marriage of Jews with Jews. One eminent scholar of marriage and family life—Professor J. H. S. Bossard—analyzed and emphasized the importance of ritual as holding
and binding families together. For the most part he was
discussing rituals with reference to everyday habits and
practices which were, as a rule, unique to a given family
and which he interpreted as having the definite result of
furthering a kind of family integration and intactness ex-
tending, sometimes, over two or more generations.

With the Jews, certain ritualistic practices which are a
part of the family pattern are also matters of concern to
the group and have the sanction of centuries. Mandelbaum
speaks of "the high value which Jews tend to place on affiliation with, and approval of, the in-group". He says that
"Jews, more than most other peoples, find personal satis-
faction in keeping up the social structure and, conversely
that the prospect of deliberately cutting oneself off from
one's Jewish affiliations awakens considerable guilt . . .and
this special weighting of the importance of the in-commu-
nity has long been true and may be one of the significant
underlying continuities in Jewish culture."[17] We have
here, then, a strong group pressure reinforcing endogamy
which, as of the moment, seems to be remarkably effec-

tive. I must repeat in closing, that there is some dimuntion in the degree of Jewish endogamy but less so—and markedly much less so—than in any other white religious or ethnic minority group.

This is impressive, I think, in a society where the pattern or trend is toward general assimilation whenever and wherever possible. In the Jewish group, we seem to have a rather clear example of a unique and distinctive kind of selective assimilation.

1. Bossard, J.H.S. and Boll, E.S., *One Marriage, Two Faiths,* 89.

2. Wouk, H., *This is My God,* 137.

3. Zborowski, M., "The Place of Book Learning in Traditional Jewish Culture", Mead, M. and Wolfenstein, M., *Childhood in Contemporary Culture,* 141.

4. Uris, Leon., *Exodus,* 197.

5. Fauman, S. J., "Occupational Selection among Detroit Jews", in Sklare, M., *The Jews,* 137.

6. Gordon, A. I., *Jews in Suburbia,* 243.

7. Barron, M., *People Who Intermarry,* p. 186.

8. *Ibid.,* 186.

9. Chancellor, L. E., & Monahan, T. P., "Religious Preferences and Interreligious Mixtures in Marriages and Divorces in Iowa", *American Sociological Review,* November, 1955, 244.

10. Gordon, *op. cit.,* p. 244.

10a. See sources in footnote 5, on p. 194.

10b. *Op. cit.*

11. Bossard and Boll, *op. cit.,* 171.

12. Robison, S., "A Study of Delinquency among Jewish Children in New York City," Sklare, *op. cit.,* 635.

13. Snyder, C. S., "Culture and Jewish Sobriety: The Ingroup-Outgroup Factor", Sklare, *op. cit.,* 560.

14. Roueche, B., "The Christian Diversion", in *The New Yorker,* January 9, 1960, 41.

15. Packard, V., *The Status Seekers,* 166.

16. *Ibid.,* 564.

17. Mandelbaum, D. G., "Change and Continuity in Jewish Life", Sklare, *op. cit.,* 511.

INTERMARRIAGE AND THE SURVIVAL
OF THE JEWISH PEOPLE

By Meir Ben-Horin

1. *Consensus*

The Central Conference of American Rabbis declared in 1909 that intermarriage was "contrary to the tradition of the Jewish religion and should therefore be discouraged by the American rabbinate." Kaufmann Kohler, president of the Hebrew Union College, wrote in his *Jewish Theology* (1928) that because of the universalistic Messianic hope "it is still imperative . . .that the Jewish people . . . continue its separateness . . . and avoid intermarrying with members of other sects."

Rabbis Frederic A. Doppelt and David Polish, in their *Guide for Reform Jews* (1957) follow through with the recommendation that "one should marry a member of our faith or one converted to our faith prior to the marriage, so that the heritage of Israel may be transmitted from generation to generation, as our Torah states, 'But you will go to my country and to my kindred, and take a wife for my son Isaac.' (Gen. 24:4)"

Herman Wouk, neo-orthodoxy's popular spokesman before the English-speaking community, refers in *This Is My God* (1959) to the problem of intermarriage under the heading, "The Assimilator Speaks." He mentions

"the girl who sued to break her grandfather's will, which barred from his legacies any grandchild marrying outside the faith. The girl's parents have given her no Jewish training. She wanted her Gentile sweetheart, and also her ancestor's stocks and bonds, but not his awkward religion. I believe she won (pp. 255-256)."

The assimilators of various kinds, says Wouk, although surviving as persons, are lost to Judaism. "The nerve of Judaism is killed in them."

The late Chief Rabbi of the British Empire, Joseph H. Hertz, in his edition of *The Pentateuch* (1936), comments on Deuteronomy 7:3,4 ("neither shalt thou make marriages with them [*i.e.*, the Canaanites]: thy daughter thou shalt not give unto his son, nor his daughter shalt thou take unto thy son, For he will turn away thy son from following Me"). Says Rabbi Hertz: "In our own days, in conditions that are worlds asunder from those in Canaan of old, intermarriage is no less fatal to the continued existence of Israel." In support he adduces this statement by Rabbi Morris Joseph of England written in 1903: "Every Jew who contemplates marriage outside the pale must regard himself as paving the way to a disruption which would be the final, as it would be the culminating, disaster in the history of his people."

Conservative Jews are no less outspoken. Chancellor Louis Finkelstein of the Jewish Theological Seminary of America puts it this way in his essay, "Jewish Religion: Its Beliefs and Practices":

"Because of the special place that the home occupies in Judaism as a center of religious life and worship, almost co-ordinate with the synagogue itself, Judaism holds it essential that both parties to a Jewish marriage be members of the Jewish faith. There is, of course, no objection to marriage with a sincere convert to Judaism. But it is not possible for the home to function in the manner prescribed by Jewish law unless both husband and wife are of the Jewish faith."

"The home has been and must continue to be a stronghold of Jewish life, hallowed by the spirit of love and reverence, by moral discipline and religious observance and worship."[1]

In *Judaism for the Modern Age* (1955) Rabbi Robert Gordis speaks of "assimilation and intermarriage" as defections from Jewry (p. 50). He indicates, however, that "there are grounds for believing that the Jewish community gains a substantial proportion of non-Jews who marry Jews." He would, then, not write off all intermarriages as defections but differentiate between intermarriages that are withdrawals from Judaism and intermarriages that are accretions to it.

Professor Mordecai M. Kaplan, on the conservative-reconstructionist side, warns in *The Future of the American Jew* (1948) against the attitude of Jews who look upon the rabbi as the person who is "paid to be a Jew" and against the Jew who has been described as "Jacob without the ladder." For it is in their homes that children may grow up unable to understand why they should not join the church to which their non-Jewish sweethearts may belong, for the sake of marriage (p. 11). In his *Questions Jews Ask: Reconstructionist Answers* (1956), Dr. Kaplan states:

"Since Jews are a minority and Judaism is exposed to

tremendous disintegrating forces from the non-Jewish environment, and since Reconstructionism is concerned with the perpetuation of Judaism, it cannot approve of uncontrolled intermarriage with non-Jews."

Those who do decide on intermarriage should, of course, not be regarded as living in immoral relationship, but "the Jewish party to the marriage is guilty of a dereliction in his or her obligation to Judaism" (p. 225). Hence, formal conversion to Judaism should be required. If the non-Jewish partner, after study and full consideration, is willing to embrace Judaism, "he should be given every encouragement and should be welcomed into the Jewish community" (p. 225).

Without attempting a real documentation, the generalization seems quite safe that Jewish survivalism, both religious and secular, is unanimous in its opposition to "uncontrolled intermarriage."

We know, of course, that Max Nordau in 1894 asked Theodor Herzl for his opinion on how the announcement of his, Nordau's, marriage to a Gentile lady might be received by the Jews, and we recall Herzl's answer:

"I do not believe that honestly and reasonably one may hold it against you. Who are we today? Citizens of the ideal Jewish State the establishment of which in the land is to us the most beautiful content of our lives. Were our work already accomplished, it would, I think, not be forbidden for a Jewish citizen, that is, a citizen of the established Jewish State, to marry a foreigner. She would thereby become politically Jewish, without regard for her religion. If there are children, they will be Jews. . . . For the rest, some striking examples could be given: if I am not mistaken, Moses was married to a Midianite."[2]

But even here, in this exchange among two extraordinary secularist Jews whose life was dedicated to the restoration of Jewish statehood and the rescue of the Jewish people from physical extinction, the underlying assumption is that in some way—politically, they call it—the family remains united within the Jewish fold.

The remarkable uniformity of opinion among Jews, normally hopelessly divided and subdivided, calls for explanation. No bi-partisan "foreign policy" here, no tri- partisans—but rather a *multipartisan,* indeed, an *omnipartisan* agreement which cannot but be rooted in the very essence of Judaism, in that which keeps together all its factions—from Buber to Beigin, from Soloveitchik to Kallen, from Lazaron to Abba Hillel Silver—in what permits it to orchestrate its disharmonies.

It is for this reason that the main portion of these thoughts on intermarriage and the Jewish future will deal with that essence.

First, however, a brief reference to statistics.

2. *Some Intermarriage Statistics*

Is intermarriage a significant problem that needs to be discussed vis-à-vis the survival of the Jewish People?

In the 1920's and 1930's Jewish intermarriage figures (in percentages) were in

Vienna	25
Budapest	28
Berlin	45
Trieste	71[3]

For the United States, studies show that at the turn of the century a percentage of 1.17 was quite insignificant. In the thirties, however, the figure for smaller communities approaches 10 per cent. Albert I. Gordon in *Jews in Suburbia (1959)* cites 7.4 per cent as the figure for native-born children of native-born parents. In Los Angeles, 7 per cent of the Jews married members of another faith. About 12 per cent of the households in the Greater Washington area are mixed. In other areas, for instance San Francisco, figures are still higher, although not yet as high as in Europe.

Clearly, intermarriage is not a figment of our imagination. It is real, as we shall hear from other discussants, on the campus, in small communities, in metropolitan areas, and elsewhere.

How shall we approach it? With what in our minds shall we view it?

The comments which follow are statements expressing the way one Jewish survivalist, with a stake in Jewish education, looks at Jewishness, at Jewish survival, and the marriage relationship. They are nothing more than footnotes to the unanimous views of the principal versions of modern Judaism.

3. *Jewish Survival Not a Foregone Conclusion*

There is nothing "in the stars" or behind the heavenly bodies which reliably guarantees our ongoing existence.

Judaism is not nature's own way of life; neither are democracy, socialism, Christianity, Americanism, Sovietism, Buddhism, pragmatism, mysticism.

Judaism is not history's own chosen system. History has been friendly and unfriendly toward a multitude of systems. In fact, history, of course, is an abstraction for varieties of events. History possesses no mind and no will of her own—just as science, religion, education, art, culture have no minds of their own. Thinking occurs in men and women, not in the abstractions which they have produced in order to achieve a measure of control over reality and to gain a measure of understanding of its flux. Jewry and Judaism are mortal like everything on earth, like the earth itself, like the solar system.

There is nothing automatic about our survival as an identifiable people. Massive, continuous efforts on our part are required to assure survival. Our strength must be conserved, replenished, augmented. Our power plants must be kept in full and growing production. Our methods must be flexible, yet effective and orderly, geared to the purpose of creative survival. Even when we make such efforts, there can be no certainty, only hope. It is, however, reasonably certain that without such efforts, hope is sheer vanity.

4. *Judaism Is Not Indispensable*

No man is indispensable to mankind—neither Moses nor Ghandhi nor Herzl. No civilization is indispensable. Cretan, Sumerian, Chaldean, Aztec cultures have vanished, yet their fading away has not reduced mankind to bestiality. In fact, advance may require a leaving behind, an overcoming, a relinquishing to oblivion. Death seems a necessity of life. Dispensability seems a condition of opportunity. Events in flux are the only stability.

To the extent that advanced civilizations are instruments of human fulfilment, they may be interchangeable. A human being may achieve fulfilment of his destiny through any one of them—American, European, Asian, Moslem, Jewish.

As civilizations become more "open," hospitable, flexible, "civilized," men may more readily and more easily shift their allegiances from civilization to civilization—just as they choose their mates, their education, their vocations and avocations, their social, political, and religious affiliations.

Judaism becomes increasingly a matter of choice rather than of birth, and choice, again, is not automatic but deliberate, calling for effort on the part of the to-be-chosen. "Laissez faire" is unreliable, possibly hazardous.

5. *Jewish Survival Requires Sustained Effort*

The fact of our extinguishability and the fact of our dispensability render modern Jewish survivalism, like survivalism throughout the ages of Jewish existence, a matter of sustained and deliberate effort aimed at neutralizing or eliminating the concrete threats and challenges that confront Judaism in our time.

Among these threats and challenges the following will have to be included:

a. Communism, which cuts off a mighty branch from Israel's tree of life;

b. Nasserism, which threatens to annihilate the Jewish state and hence diverts precious energies of Israel and the Jewish people united with Israel into unproductive channels;

c. Neo-nazism in its various forms, which undermines Jewish recuperation from nazism and the Jewish sense of security in the postwar world;

d. Urbanization or metropolitanization, which concentrates the majority of our people in "profitable" target areas for nuclear strikes;

e. Percentual reduction through the world population explosion, which favors the non-Jewish "huddled masses" of mankind;

f. A lull or nadir in philosophical and religious creativity of which some recent neo-mystical and existentialist writings may be the evidence, not the refutation;

g. A certain erosion of the "will to endure"—which culminates in assimilation, intermarriage, withdrawal, and "failure of nerve."

h. An inadequate, because largely elementary, system of education. "Spiritually," Pope Pius XI had said, "we are all Semites." But we "Semites" do not become "spiritual": we become merely—"Bar Mitzvah." Ours is a widespread failure to attain crucial understandings of Judaism.

6. *Jewish Survival Requires Basic Understandings*

Since it cannot rely on nature, on history, on cultural "laissez faire," Jewish survivalism requires certain basic understandings about Judaism and certain conditions of existence.

Among these understandings are the following:

a. An understanding, by Jews and non-Jews alike, that Jewish destructability is a form of human destructability and, hence, that defending and protecting Jewish life or any life is guarding and securing the sanctity and untouchability of human life as such. Human destructability dictates not greater pugnacity but greater human solidarity and better security measures for man's life.

By guarding Jewish life and existence, we man our sector of the human frontline against evil. No soldier can do better than give his all for his sector of the front.

Our destructability calls for maximal efforts to make us as indestructable as humanly possible.

b. An understanding by Jews that Jewish dispensability really spells Jewish indispensability. The fact that men and cultures are unique transforms equal dispensability into equal indispensability. We are all equally dispensable and, therefore, being human, we are all equally indispensable. A human life is holy no matter how dispensable it may be. It cannot be wiped out without penalty. A civilization, unique and immensely precious, enriching for all, is no less indispensable because it is mortal and dispensable. As far as we Jews are concerned, Judaism is as indispensable to us as American civilization is to Americans, as western civilization is to western man — as we are to ourselves. Judaism is equally dispensable to any other civilization and, hence, it is equally indispensable.[4]

c. An understanding of what Judaism is, how it came to be what it is, and where it may go in the future. A tentative formulation to serve as hypothesis for inquiry may define Judaism as the religious civilization and civilizing religion of the Jewish people or, perhaps better, —the Jewish people's civilization of "the religious," centering in faith in the promise of existence and seeking to make it manifest in the life of mankind.[5]

Judaism may be understood, if the foregoing is to be amplified a bit further, as a bold experiment in human association, as a fruitful hypothesis of man's spirituality. Judaism may be taken as a worthwhile, history-tested, experience-drenched attempt at making manifest the promise that resides in the dimension of space, time, and life.

Judaism, in sum, may be seen as the Jewish people's way of expressing man's distinctive nature as a *homebuilder, homo faber domus,* a transformer of earth and the heavens into a human abode, into man's "home." Judaism may be felt and grasped to be the Jewish people's way of "homebuilding" on a local, national, global, and cosmic scale—or as its quest for salvation.[6]

d. An understanding not only of what Judaism is but how it functions, how it pursues its fulfilment as a "homebuilding" civilization.

It is at this point that the remarkable unanimity among Jews in their opposition to what Rabbi Kaplan has called "uncontrolled intermarriage" becomes intelligible.

7. *The Meaning of Judaism and of Marriage*

In order to attain its fulfilment as a "homebuilding" civilization, Judaism requires its *home-land,* which is Israel, its *home-centers* or the organized Jewish communities in many lands, and—above all—its *home-bases,* that is, the family units or "homes of homes."

Jewish history has been described as the Jewish people's way from Zion to Zion.[7] This holds much truth when "Zion" is taken to refer to the Jewish state. A still greater truth is so stated when "Zion" is understood to refer to the totality of "homebuildership" to which Judaism is dedicated—familial, national, all-human, and cosmic. For Judaism, in this sense of multi-dimensional Zionism, indeed is the Jewish people's way from Zion to Zion, from the Jewish home "at home" to the Jewish home at the core of existence.

What, then, is this *home-base,* this "home of homes," this family unit established through the institution of marriage? What is a marriage?

The answer is that marriage is an "I for an I," a conjugation of two egos, a union of woman and man for the purpose, not simply of procreation or economic security or self-satisfaction, but for the purpose of making manifest the promise of existence in two human beings. Marriage is a civilization's institution for making manifest the promise of existence that inheres in its most basic human relationship. It is the foundational institution of its homebuildership or "Zionism." It is the launching site for its flight to fulfilment. It is the ground-floor laboratory for its chief propositions. Together with its schools, it is the Canaveral of a civilization's profoundest wisdom regarding the ways of man to God and God to man.

Stated differently, it is a civilization's "little Zion." To paraphrase a rabbinic saying, the family—like a wife—is an *ezer ke-negdo: zakhah*—and it is a "little Zion," *lo zakhah*

—and it is a "Little Rock" (with huge problems of integration).

Conclusion

Judaism, in order to live, must require the fullest loyalty to itself on all levels of homebuilding or Zionist realization.

As the Jewish people's way of life and way to life, Judaism, bent on continuity and creative transformation, cannot surrender its claim upon the most private of all concerns—the family. For all its homebuilding is mere dream and reverie without the home's home. Of its families it must demand that they say, not only "I am *with* you," not only, "I am *for* you," but—"I am *of* you," that is, I am as Jewish as you are.[8]

Deuteronomy 6:5 records Moses' admonition which has accompanied Israel on its historic sojourn: "Thou shalt love the Lord thy God with all thy heart and with all thy soul and with all *meodekha*," thy strength, power, might. Some rabbis interpreted it as substance, financial power. In the context of the foregoing discussion, one may be permitted to interpret it, by switching the letters of *meod,* as—*adam,* manpower. Hence, "thou shalt love thy Lord thy God with all thy heart," that is, with your emotions, your capacity for love; "and with all thy soul," that is, your capacity for thought; "and with all thy *meod*"— your humanity, your men, women and children, the strength of your manhood and womanhood, your capacity to be human, that is, your capacity to build homes, Jewish homes, those "little Zions" from which there goes forth the Law, the "little Jerusalems" from which breaks forth the Word of the Lord calling upon us to move forward from one "Zion" to the next.

1. Louis Finkelstein, "Jewish Religion: Its Beliefs and Practices," *The Jews, Their History, Culture, and Religion* (New York: Harper & Brothers Publishers, 3rd edition, 1960), vol. ii, 1741, 1758.

2. Anna et Maxa Nordau, *Max Nordau, L'homme, le penseur, le sioniste* (Paris: La Terre Retrouvée, 1948), 99.

3. Aryeh Tartakower, *Ha-hebrah ha-yehudith* (Jewish Society) (Tel-Aviv: Massadah, 1957), 217.

4. *See* Meir Ben-Horin, "Judaism in a Natural Key," *Jewish Spectator*, New York, vol. xxi, no. 10 (December 1956).

5. *See idem*, "Civilization of 'The Religious,' " *Studies and Essays* in honor of President Abraham A. Newman (Philadelphia: Dropsie College Press, 1962), 49-87.

6. *See* Meir Ben-Horin, *Max Nordau, Philosopher of Human Solidarity* (New York: Conference on Jewish Social Studies, 1957), 50 f. and *idem*, "Reconsidering Max Nordau" in Raphael Patai, editor, *Herzl Year Book*, Vol. ii (New York: Herzl Press, 1959) 153-170.

7. Zeev Jabotinsky, *Golah we-hitboleluth* (Diaspora and Assimilation) (Tel-Aviv: S. Saltzman, 1936), 334-340; also in *idem, Zamelbukh* (Buenos Aires: New Zionist Organization of Argentina, 1939), 9-15.

8. *See* Meir Ben-Horin, "Jewishness and the Jew," *The Reconstructionist*, New York, vol. xxvi, no. 3 (March 18, 1960), 9-14.

FACTS AS WE KNOW THEM

INTERFAITH MARRIAGE IN SWITZERLAND

By Jacob Baar and Werner J. Cahnman

In view of the dearth of statistical information on inter-faith marriage in the United States, it appears desirable to review the data available on the marriage of Jews and non-Jews in European countries. As an example, we have chosen Switzerland, one of the few European countries which was not affected by World Wars I and II. As in the United States, the Swiss Jews are chiefly urban dwellers and engaged in business and in the professions. About one half of them are the descendants of families who resided for generations either in Switzerland or in the German and French-speaking areas adjacent to Switzerland, and they are thoroughly acculturated.[1] But even the other half, who are of East-European origin, are mostly natives of Switzerland. It should be pointed out, however, that the Swiss, in general, have not been as hospitable to people of divergent origins as have Americans. Perhaps an even more important difference is that the number of Jews in Switzerland is only an insignificant fraction of the number residing in the United States, and that compactly settled Jewish neighborhoods are entirely lacking in Switzerland.

The Jews never accounted for more than ½ of 1 percent of the total population of Switzerland. They numbered little more than 8,000 in 1888 and increased to a maximum of about 21,000 in 1920, just after World War I. As Table 1 shows, the Jewish population was down to about 19,000 by 1950, the latest year for which data are presently available. It is apparent also, from the lower tier of the table, that there is not much disparity in the number of males and females. In each sex, about two fifths of the Jews are recorded as alien residents, reflecting the reluctance of the Swiss government to confer citizenship on the Jewish population. Children do not acquire citizenship at birth in Switzerland if their parents are aliens.

As in the United States, the Jewish population in Switzerland tends to concentrate in certain areas. According to the latest figures, about one third of the Swiss Jews

Table 1
(A)

Jewish Population of Switzerland[2]

Year	Number of Jews	Number per 1,000 Total Population
1888	8,069	3
1900	12,264	4
1910	18,462	5
1920	20,979	5
1930	17,973	4
1941	19,429	5
1950	19,048	4

Table 1

(B)

Number of Jews Who Are

	Swiss Citizens		Alien Residents	
	Male	Female	Male	Female
1910	3,256	3,019	6,107	6,080
1920	4,862	4,566	5,705	5,846
1930	5,028	4,775	3,987	4,183
1941	5,143	5,136	4,775	4,375
1950	5,227	5,508	4,243	4,070

reside in Zurich and an additional third in Geneva and Basel. Next in order are Vaud (Lausanne) with about 1,800 Jewish residents and Bern with 1,400.[3]

The intermarriage of Jews with those of other faiths has been steadily increasing in Switzerland, and is probably representative of the experience in other countries where the process of acculturation has continued over a considerable period of time. Table 2 shows in some detail the trend of interfaith marriage at successive census periods. Thus, in 1888 no less than 97.4 percent of the Jewish husbands in Switzerland were married to Jewish wives. By 1950 the proportion had dropped to 80.6 percent. In other words, the proportion of Jewish husbands living in interfaith marriages increased from 2.6 to 19.4 percent in this period. Similarly, Jewish women in Switzerland have been intermarrying with increasing frequency, although not to the same extent as the men. In 1888, only 2.9 percent of Jewish wives were married to non-Jews, practically the same figure as for Jewish husbands; in 1950, the proportion was 10 percent, or only half that for husbands.

Table 2

Interfaith Marriage of Jews in Switzerland[4]

Year	Percent of Jewish Husbands Whose Wives Are				Percent of Jewish Wives Whose Husbands Are			
	Jewish	Protestant	Catholic	Other	Jewish	Protestant	Catholic	Other
				Total Population				
1888	97.4	1.4	1.0	.2	97.1	1.4	0.9	0.6
1900	95.9	2.4	1.6	.1	96.9	1.8	1.0	0.3
1910	95.1	3.0	1.7	.2	95.7	2.4	1.0	0.9
1920	93.1	3.8	2.8	.3	94.6	3.2	1.3	0.9
1930	90.8	5.5	3.0	.7	92.3	4.5	2.0	1.2
1941	87.5	7.6	4.2	.7	93.1	4.6	1.6	0.7
1950	80.6	11.1	6.8	1.5	90.0	6.3	2.5	1.2
				Swiss Citizens				
1910	95.8	3.1	1.1	-	94.5	4.1	0.5	0.9
1920	93.0	4.1	2.7	.2	92.6	5.0	1.3	1.1
1930	90.9	5.7	2.8	.6	90.1	6.1	2.4	1.4
1941	86.5	8.4	4.4	.7	90.6	6.8	1.7	0.9
1950	79.8	12.3	6.7	1.2	87.4	8.8	2.7	1.1
				Alien Residents				
1910	94.7	2.9	2.0	.4	96.5	1.2	1.3	1.0
1930	93.2	3.5	3.0	.3	96.7	1.2	1.3	0.8
1941	90.7	5.0	3.3	1.0	96.3	1.7	1.2	0.8
1920	89.2	6.3	3.8	.7	96.9	1.3	1.5	0.3
1950	82.2	9.0	6.8	2.0	94.7	1.9	2.3	1.1

Throughout the period under review, Jews who married outside their faith showed a considerably greater preference for Protestant than for Catholic spouses. It is apparent from Table 2 that this is true for both men and women. In 1950, for example, 11.1 percent of the Jewish husbands had Protestant wives and 6.8 percent had Catholic spouses. For Jewish women, the corresponding proportions were 6.3 and 2.5 percent. The fact that the Jewish population in Switzerland is largely concentrated in areas predominantly Protestant undoubtedly plays a major role in the differential intermarriage rates.

The proportion of Jews married to Protestants has been consistently greater among those who are Swiss citizens than among those who are alien residents. This tendency is more sharply defined in cases where the wife is Jewish than in families where the husband is Jewish. In 1950, for instance, 8.8 percent of the Jewish wives were married to Protestants in citizen families but the proportion was only 1.9 percent in families where the spouses were aliens. For Jewish-Catholic couples, however, citizenship seemed to make little difference.

Table 3

Interfaith Marriages of Jews Performed in Switzerland[5]

Years	Total Number of Marriages	Interfaith Marriages		Religion of Spouse		
		No.	% of Total	Protestant	Catholic	Other
Groom Jewish						
1946-50	982	414	42.2	256	141	17
1951-55	728	322	44.2	184	129	9
1956-60	638	299	46.9	168	122	9
Bride Jewish						
1946-50	699	131	18.7	78	47	6
1951-55	515	109	21.2	70	30	9
1956-60	593	127	21.4	66	49	12

Our analysis thus far has been based on information gathered in census years, generally about 10 years apart. Such data show the statistical picture at successive periods of time, but do not indicate the year-to-year variations in interfaith marriage. The annual figures, reported in the vital statistics, are given in Table 3. It should be noted that these figures are based on the number of marriages — not on the number of individuals — and hence are about twice as high as the percentages given in the preceding tables.

Table 3 shows even more dramatically than the census data the extent of intermarriage. In the years 1956-60, not far from half of the marriages in Switzerland in which the groom was Jewish the bride was non-Jewish. In the same period, more than one fifth of the Jewish brides married out of their faith. In both sexes the proportion has been steadily rising. This does not augur well for the continued viability of the Jewish community in Switzerland. However, in comparing the Swiss picture to the prospects in the United States, the vastly greater number of Jews living in major American population centers must be taken into consideration.

Notes

1. Among the oldest Swiss Jewish families are the Guggenheims, whose name is derived from a small place between Frankfurt and Heidelberg. For the American branch of that family, see Harvey O'Connor, The Guggenheims — The Making of an American Dynasty. (New York, 1937)

2. Quellenwerke der Schweiz, Heft 288, p. 75.

3. For more detailed statistical and historical information on the Jews in Switzerland, see Kurt B. Mayer, "The Population of Switzerland" (New York 1952); Hans Guth, "Die Juden in der Schweiz im Spiegel der Bevoelkerungsstatistik," Schweizerischer Israelitischer Gemeindebund, Festschrift zum 50 Jaehrigen Bestehen (Zurich 1954); Guido Kisch, "The Jews in Switzerland," Historia Judaica, Vol. XIV, October 1952, Part 2, 159-162.

4. Quellenwerke der Schweiz, Heft 288, p. 83.

5. Statistisches Jahrbuch der Schweiz, 1961, p. 48.

INTERMARRIAGE IN CANADA 1921-1960
by Louis Rosenberg

I

While the primary purpose of this study is to analyze the extent of intermarriage among Jews in Canada during the period from 1921 to 1960, the Canadian data presented are not only interesting in themselves, but can have also considerable significance for the understanding of the situation in other English speaking countries, and particularly in the neighboring Jewish community in the United States, for which adequate official statistical information is not available.

Although Jewish settlement in North America, and resettlement in England, dates back more than 300 years and the bicentenary of Jewish settlement in Canada was celebrated in 1959, the Jewish community in Canada is of comparatively recent date. In its origin, composition, structure and cultural pattern it is largely the product of a series of waves of Jewish migration from Eastern and Central Europe commencing in 1882 and, with interruption during World War II, continuing until the early 1950's.

As in the United States, Jewish immigration into Canada followed the pogroms and political persecutions in Europe. It is noteworthy, however, that about 42 percent of all Jewish immigrants into Canada since 1901 arrived there after 1921, when immigration into the United States, owing to the quota legislation adopted in 1921 and 1924, fell off sharply. Still more significant is the fact that about 66 percent of these post-1921 immigrants arrived after 1945. As a result, the Canadian Jewish Community is considerable younger than the Jewish community in the United States.

Canada is the only country in the English speaking world where detailed and reliable statistical information about the Jewish population and its demographic characteristics is available. This is of distinct advantage in comparision especially to the United States, where one has to rely on private surveys which are of necessity based on uncertain data and unrepresentative samples.

Official statistical information regarding ethnic origin and religious affiliation in Canada is not confined to the decennial census, which has compiled such statistics since 1851. The annual reports on vital statistics compiled by the Dominion Bureau of Statistics from 1921 onwards, which are based on uniform statistical reports furnished by the Departments of Vital Statistics of Canada's provincial governments, give the ethnic origin and sex of all children born each year and the ethnic origin and age of the mothers, along with all deaths classified by ethnic origin for the period from 1926 to 1951. Unfortunately, the statistical information concerning births and deaths, cross-classified by ethnic origin, was discontinued at the request of the provincial governments after 1951, but statistical information concerning all marriages in Canada and each of its provinces, cross-classified by the religion of bride and groom, has been compiled by the Department of Vital Statistics of the Dominion Bureau of Statistics for all provinces, except Quebec, for the years 1921 to 1925, and for all provinces including Quebec for the years 1926 to 1960. This statistical information, kindly made available to the writer each year by the Department of Vital Statistics, has made the present study of intermarriage among Jews in Canada possible.

There is no official statistical information available concerning the religion of brides and grooms married in Great Britain, South Africa or Australia. In the United States such information has been available only for the State of Iowa since 1953 and for the State of Indiana since 1959. This makes the Canadian data all the more valuable.

Intermarriage is defined in this paper as a marital union, with the religion reported by one spouse at the time of marriage differing from that reported by the other spouse. A marriage in which the Jewish spouse has been converted to Christianity before marriage or a marriage in which the non-Jewish spouse has been converted to Judaism before marriage is not considered an intermarriage.

The intermarriage or out-marriage, rates given in this study are therefore minimal rates, in as far as they do not include cases where one of the spouses has undergone nominal conversion to the religion of the other spouse prior to marriage, but does not become or remain a sincere and observant member of the religious faith adopted after the marriage has been consumated.

In comparing the intermarriage rates of Jews in Canada with those in the United States, it must be borne in mind that such American data as are available are derived from local or sample surveys, compiled in a few selected areas, and that people identifying themselves therein as Jews have done so voluntarily, thereby permitting an unknown and perhaps substantial number of Jews who have intermarried and who have cut all ties with the Jewish community to deny their Jewish origin and thus to escape statistical identification. In contradistinction, the intermarriage rate of Jews in Canada is based on all-inclusive and official national and provincial marriage statistics compiled annually by the Department of Vital Statistics of the Canadian Government. If one takes further into consideration other factors, especially the one that the Canadian Jewish community is younger and less acculturated than the one in the United States, certain conclusions from the data become permissible.

Methods of calculating the rate of intermarriage differ; and for purposes of comparison with intermarriage rates in other countries it is therefore important to clearly state the method used in this study.

The intermarriage rate is calculated by finding the percentage which those intermarried form of the total number of marriages in which one or both parties to the marriage were Jewish. This is quite simple when the intermarriage rate for men or for women is being calculated. A difficulty develops, however, when the percentage of intermarriage for the total Jewish population of both sexes is being calculated.

There are two possible methods which may be used: a) The intermarriage rate is based upon the percentage of intermarriage among all couples in which one or both parties to the marriage are Jewish, (Method "A"), or b) The intermarriage rate is based upon the percentage of intermarriage among all Jewish individuals, i.e. the total number of Jewish grooms and Jewish brides (Method "B").[1]

In the example presented in note 1, the intermarriage

rate as calculated by Method "A" would be 15.6 percent, as compared with 8.5 percent by Method "B". The difference results from the fact that Method "A" gives the percentage of intermarried couples among Jews, while Method "B" gives the percentage of Jewish individuals intermarried. Since a marriage necessarily involves two persons, the writer is inclined to prefer method "A", but method "B" is used by the Dominion Bureau of Statistics in the article on intermarriage in the annual volume of the Canada Year Book and the same method has been used by other authors in dealing with this subject. Method "B" will therefore be used consistently throughout this study in order to facilitate comparison with intermarriage rates in other countries.

II

In Table I will be found the comparative intermarriage rates for the total population and each of the sexes among Jews, Catholics and Protestants in Canada in each of the quinquennial periods from 1926 to 1960. In calculating these intermarriage rates we have included among Protestants all non-Catholic Christian denominations, and among Catholics we have included Roman Catholics and Greek Catholics.

It should further be noted that although there are marriage statistics available for the other provinces of Canada for the period from 1921 to 1925, there are no such statistics available during that period for the province of Quebec.

It will be noted that the rate of intermarriages among Jews, Protestants and Catholics has steadily increased in every quinquennial period from 1926 to 1960, both for men and for women. Although the rate of intermarriage is higher among Protestants than among Jews, and highest among Catholics, the increase in the rate of intermarriage

TABLE I

Comparative Intermarriage Rates among Jews, Protestants and Catholics in Canada in Quinquennial Periods

	BOTH SEXES			MEN			WOMEN		
	Jews	Prot- estants	Cath- olics	Jews	Prot- estants	Cath- olics	Jews	Prot- estants	Cath- olics
1926-30	2.5	5.3	8.4	3.7	5.9	7.2	1.3	4.8	9.2
1931-35	2.6	6.5	9.8	3.2	7.1	8.5	1.9	5.9	11.0
1936-40	3.2	6.9	8.8	4.3	7.5	8.1	2.0	5.8	10.0
1941-45	5.0	8.1	10.3	6.6	8.8	9.3	3.4	7.5	11.2
1946-50	4.8	8.9	10.8	6.6	9.4	10.2	2.9	8.4	11.8
1951-55	6.2	10.2	11.3	8.5	10.5	11.0	3.8	9.9	12.1
1956-60	7.6	11.1	11.7	10.0	11.3	11.3	4.8	10.8	12.1

in the entire period from 1926 to 1960 has been greater among Jews than among either Protestants or Catholics. The quiquennial intermarriage rate has increased three-fold among Jews, namely from 2.5 percent in 1926-30 to 7.6 percent in 1956-1960, as compared with slightly more than two-fold from 5.3 percent to 11.1 percent among Protestants, and only 27 percent, namely from 8.4 percent to 11.7 percent, among Catholics.

The intermarriage rate among Jews in Canada was more than twice as high among Jewish men than among Jewish women in each of the quinquennial periods since 1926, except in the periods 1931-35 and 1941-46, while the intermarriage rate among Protestants was from 12 to 30 percent higher among men than among women in the period from 1926 to 1930, and only 4 percent higher in the period from 1956 to 1960. Among Catholics, the intermarriage rate was higher among women than among men in each of the quinquennial periods, although the percentage by which the intermarriage rate among Catholic women exceeded that among Catholic men has decreased in each quinquennial period from 1926-30 to 1956-60.

The highest intermarriage rate among men and women in Canada in any one of the years from 1926 to 1960 was 11.9 percent in 1955 among Catholics, 11.6 percent among Protestants in 1960, and 8.9 percent among Jews in 1959, while among men the highest intermarriage rate in any year was 12.2 percent among Jews in 1959, 11.9 percent among Protestants in 1957, and 11.5 percent among Catholics in 1960. Among women the highest intermarriage rate in any year was 12.5 percent among Catholics in 1955, 11.5 percent among Protestants in 1960, and 6.1 percent among Jews in 1960. It is evident from these statistics that while the intermarriage rate in Canada was three times as high among all Catholics than among all Jews, and slightly less than twice as high among all Protestants than among all Jews in 1926, it was almost the same among Jewish men as among either Catholic or Protestant men in the two year period from 1959 to 1960; the only reason why the total intermarriage rate among Jews in Canada in the period from 1954 to 1960 was lower than among Catholics or Protestants was the very low rate of intermarriage among Jewish women as compared with the intermarriage rate among Catholic and Protestant women.

The intermarriage rate among Jews is by no means uniform throughout Canada. It is much lower in Quebec than in Ontario and Manitoba, and even lower than in Saskatchewan and Alberta, the Atlantic provinces of Nova Scotia, New Brunswick and Newfoundland, and the Pacific coast province of British Columbia.

In Table II will be found the number of all marriages as well as the number and percentage of intermarriages among Jewish men in Canada and its provinces in each of the quinquennial periods from 1921 to 1960; Table

III contains the corresponding information for all marriages and intermarriages among Jewish men and women during the same period.

The highest number and percentage of intermarriages among all Jews in Canada occurred in the quinquennial period from 1956 to 1960; the rate of intermarriage among all Jews, men and women, increased from 1.9 percent in 1928 to a peak of 8.9 percent in 1959.

The rate of intermarriage among all Jews, men and women, was lowest in the province of Quebec in each of the quinquennial periods, ranging from a low of 1.5 percent in 1926-35 to a comparative high of 3.8 percent in 1956-50. This low intermarriage rate among the Jews in Quebec may be attributed to a large extent to the fact that 98.1 percent of all Jews in the province of Quebec live in Metropolitan Montreal, which is the largest Jewish community in Canada. Its Jewish population forms 40.4 percent of the total Jewish population of Canada. Moreover, the overwhelming majority of the population of Quebec is Roman Catholic by religion and French in language and culture, while the Jews, especially in Montreal, are attached to the Protestant and English speaking group, as far as linguistic usage and educational affiliation are concerned. The vast majority of the Jews of Quebec speak either English or Yiddish or both; the number of French speaking Jews is comparatively small.

There are no non-denominational public schools in Quebec. The majority of the Jewish school children attend the schools of the Protestant school system to which all Jewish school taxes are paid; in certain areas the majority of the children attending the Protestant schools are Jewish. Other Jewish children attend Jewish day schools, which give instruction in English and either Hebrew or Yiddish and are not tax supported. In other words, the cleavage which exists in Quebec between French Catholics and English Protestants facilitates the expression of a separate Jewish ethnicity and culture while, at the same time, the linguistic and educational affiliation of the Jewish population with the English-Protestant minority increases the social distance between the Jews and the French speaking majority.

The intermarriage rate among Jews in the provinces of Ontario and Manitoba is about twice as high as that in Quebec, ranging in Ontario from 2.2 percent in 1926-30 to 8.9 percent in 1956-60, and in Manitoba from 2.4 percent in 1926-30 to 6.6 percent in 1956-60. In Manitoba 96.9 percent of the Jewish population lives in Metropolitan Winnipeg, and in Ontario 81.1 percent of the Jewish population lives in MetropolitanToronto. In both Toronto and Winnipeg the majority of the Jewish children attend the non-denominational tax-supported public schools. While ethnic cleavage plays no role in these two provinces, the concentration of the Jewish population in metropolitan areas is comparable to the one in Quebec.

The picture is entirely different in the two prairie provinces of Saskatchewan and Alberta, where the intermarriage rate among all Jews, men and women, ranged from 5.9 percent in 1926-30 to a high of 23.1 percent in 1956-60. The two largest Jewish communities in Saskatchewan are in the cities of Regina and Saskatoon, and the Jewish population in these two cities does not comprise more than 31 percent of the total Jewish population in the province. In Saskatchewan, as in Ontario and Manitoba, Jewish children attend the nonconominational tax-supported public schools. More than 40 percent of the total Jewish population in this province live in towns and villages with a Jewish population of less than 100 persons and many of these very small communities cannot hire a rabbi or maintain a Hebrew school. The dispersed settlement and the concomitant acculturation to the style of life of the majority of the population no doubt account to a large extent for the higher rate of intermarriage in the prairie provinces.

The two largest Jewish communities in the province of Alberta are in the cities of Calgary and Edmonton. The Jewish population in these two cities does not form more than 48 percent of the total Jewish population in the province. There are two Jewish congregations in each of these two cities, and a large number of Jewish children attend Hebrew and Yiddish Day schools while the rest attend the non-denominational tax-supported public schools. It is of interest to note that, while the intermarriage rate among Jews in Alberta is higher than in Manitoba, Ontario and Quebec, it is lower than in the neighboring province of Saskachewan, where the largest Jewish communities are much smaller than in the province of Alberta.

In the Atlantic provinces of Nova Scotia, New Brunswick and Newfoundland, which we combine because of the smallness of the Jewish population, the intermarriage rate among all Jews, men and women, has fluctuated from a low of 5.1 percent in 1936-40 to a high of 20.4 percent in 1956-40. Halifax is the only city within this area whose Jewish population exceeds 1,000 persons. They comprise 32 percent of the total Jewish population in the three Atlantic provinces of Canada. Again, sparsity of settlement would seem to be a factor in intermarriage.

In the province of British Columbia the intermarriage rate among all Jews, men and women, ranged from 13.0 percent in 1931-35 to a high of 26.8 percent in 1956-60. This is the highest rate among Jews in any province of Canada. Vancouver is the largest Jewish community in British Columbia, and the fourth largest Jewish community in Canada. Its Jewish population, which was only 205 in 1901, has increased rapidly from 1,370 in 1921 to 7,374 in 1960 and now forms 93.4 percent of the total Jewish

Table II

Number of all marriages and number of percentage of intermarriages among Jewish men in Canada and its Provinces in each of the Quinquennial Periods from 1921 to 1960.

Quinquennial Period	Canada	Atlantic Provinces	Quebec	Ontario	Manitoba	Sask. & Alta.	B.C.
Total All Marriages							
1921-25	2.978*	95	*	1,942	654	205	82
1926-30	6,749	95	2,656	2,904	728	268	98
1931-35	7,521	84	3,088	3,222	820	213	94
1936-40	8,953	146	3,665	3,570	1,085	324	163
1941-45	9,479	191	3,838	3,924	965	308	253
1946-50	10,855	154	4,446	4,476	1,096	364	319
1951-55	9,185	116	3,682	3,931	871	292	293
1956-60	8,132	97	3,417	3,517	640	209	252
1921-60	63,852	978	24,792	27,486	6,859	2,183	1,554
Number of Intermarriages							
1921-25	155*	11	*	78	23	24	19
1926-30	250	18	63	102	26	22	19
1931-35	237	6	59	97	32	29	14
1936-40	386	12	84	159	48	37	46
1941-45	624	52	112	265	66	65	64
1946-50	711	16	166	290	84	63	92
1951-55	783	24	147	392	78	59	83
1956-60	828	25	192	405	58	66	82
1921-60	3,974	164	823	1,788	415	365	419
Percentage of Intermarriage							
1921-25	5.2*	11.6	*	4.1	3.5	11.7	23.2
1926-30	3.7	17.1	2.4	3.5	3.6	8.2	19.4
1931-35	3.2	7.1	1.9	3.0	3.9	13.6	14.9
1936-40	4.3	8.2	2.3	4.5	4.4	11.4	28.2
1941-45	6.6	27.2	2.9	6.5	6.9	21.1	25.3
1946-50	6.6	12.3	3.7	6.5	7.7	17.3	28.8
1951-55	8.5	20.7	3.9	10.0	9.0	20.2	28.3
1956-60	10.0	25.8	5.6	11.7	9.1	34.8	32.2
1921-60	6.2	16.8	3.3	6.5	6.1	16.7	27.0

*No statistics available for Quebec in 1921-25. Atlantic provinces include Nova Scotia, New Brunswick and Prince Edward Island for the years 1921-60 and the province of Newfoundland for 1946-60.

Sask. and Alta. are abbreviations for the provinces of Saskatchewan and Alberta. B.C. = British Columbia.

Table III

Number of all marriages and number and percentage of intermarriages among Jewish women in Canada and its Provinces in each of the Quinquennial Periods from 1921 to 1960.

Total All Marriages

Period							
1921-25	2,893*	87	*	1,902	642	191	71
1926-30	6,587	93	2,601	2,839	711	254	89
1931-35	7,437	85	3,062	3,180	814	206	90
1936-40	8,743	137	3,628	3,484	1,062	301	131
1941-45	9,171	155	3,796	3,792	938	269	221
1946-50	10,445	141	4,370	4,315	1,036	316	267
1951-55	8,731	95	3,619	3,700	811	264	242
1956-60	7,670	84	3,287	3,305	606	163	225
1921-60	61,677	877	24,363	26,517	6,620	1,964	1,336

Number of Intermarriages

Period							
1921-25	70*	3	*	38	11	10	8
1926-30	88	6	18	37	9	8	10
1931-35	153	7	33	55	26	22	10
1936-40	176	3	47	73	25	14	14
1941-45	316	16	70	133	39	26	32
1946-50	301	6	87	129	24	15	40
1951-55	329	4	76	161	33	21	34
1956-60	366	11	62	203	24	20	46
1921-60	1,799	56	393	829	191	136	194

Percentage of Intermarriage

Period							
1921-25	2.4*	3.5	*	2.0	1.4	5.2	11.3
1926-30	1.3	6.5	0.7	1.3	1.3	3.1	11.2
1931-35	2.1	8.2	1.1	1.7	3.2	10.7	11.1
1936-40	2.0	2.3	1.3	2.1	2.4	4.7	10.7
1941-45	3.4	9.7	1.8	3.5	4.2	9.7	14.5
1946-50	2.9	4.3	2.0	3.0	2.3	4.7	15.0
1951-55	3.8	4.2	2.1	4.4	4.0	8.0	14.0
1956-60	4.8	14.3	1.9	6.1	4.0	13.2	20.4
1921-60	2.9	6.5	1.6	3.1	2.9	6.9	14.5

*No statistics available for Quebec in 1921-25. Atlantic Provinces include Nova Scotia, New Brunswick and Prince Edward Island for the year 1921-60 and Newfoundland for 1946-60. Sask. & Alta. are abbreviations for the provinces of Saskatchewan and Alberta, B.C. = British Columbia population of British Columbia. However, it must not be overlooked that Vancouver is separated from the other Jewish communities in Canada by the vast expanse of the Rocky Mountains and that it is located more than 1500 miles west of Winnipeg, the city which has the third largest Jewish community in Canada; Winnipeg, in turn, is far distant from the main Jewish centers in Toronto and Montreal. In the past Vancouver has had closer social contacts with the American Jewish communities of Seattle, Portland and San Francisco than with the remainder of the Jewish communities in Canada. But Seattle, Portland and San Francisco were themselves exposed to similar environmental influences as Vancouver.

We turn now to the difference in intermarriage rates among Jewish men and among Jewish women. Among Jewish men the rate of intermarriage ranged from a low of 2.6 percent in 1933 to a high of 12.2 percent in 1959 in Canada as a whole. It fluctuated from a low of 1.4 percent in 1933 to a high of 7.3 percent in 1960 in Quebec. In the province of Ontario the intermarriage rate ranged from a low of 2.3 percent in 1926 to a high of 13.5 percent in 1959 and in Manitoba from a low of 2.7 percent in 1929 to a high of 13.2 percent in 1955.

In British Columbia it fluctuated from a low of 5.6 percent in 1928 to a high of 36.7 percent in 1959; in Saskatchewan and Alberta from a low of 4.3 percent in 1927 to a high of 40.0 percent in 1958; and in the Atlantic provinces from low of 3.2 percent in 1946 to a high of 33.3 percent in 1959.

Among Jewish women the rate of intermarriage ranged from a low of 0.8 percent in 1927 to a high of 6.1 percent in 1960 in Canada as a whole. It fluctuated from a low of 0.3 percent in 1929 to a high of 3.6 percent in 1946 in Quebec. In the province of Ontario it ranged from a low of 1.1

percent in 1934 to a high of 8.2 percent in 1960, and in
Manitoba from a low of 0.7 percent to a high of 6.0 percent in 1945. In British Columbia it rose from none in 1929
and 1934 to a high of 25.6 percent in 1958; in Saskatchewan and Alberta from none in 1923 and 1930 to a high
of 20.8 percent in 1960; and in the Atlantic provinces
from none in each of the years 1921, 1922, 1924, 1928,
1934, 1950, 1952 and 1953 to a high of 25.0 percent in
1960.

The difference in the rate of out-marriage between Jewish men and women is a phenomenon which is not restrict-
ed to Canada. At least in recent decades Jewish men in
various countries have out-married more frequently than
Jewish women. Among a number of contributing factors,
the sex ratio may first come to mind. For instance, the
greater number of Jewish men than Jewish women in
British Columbia, Saskatchewan, Alberta, New Brunswick
and Nova Scotia is one reason for the relatively high out-
marriage rate of Jewish men in these provinces. However,
the fact that the intermarriage rate was higher among
Jewish men in Manitoba, with a sex ratio in 1951 of 993
males per 1,000 females, than in Quebec and Ontario, with
a sex ratio of 1,023 males per 1,000 females, shows that
other factors, for instance the degree of isolation of a Jewish community, may intervene. Another consideration is
that girls are likely to be more attached to their families
and more closely supervised by them, than boys; this is
certainly true among Jews. Furthermore, Jewish men, on
the whole, are more acculturated to the general environment than are Jewish women, especially in a country like
Canada, where Jewish settlement is of relatively recent
date. Whether in business or in the professions, Jewish
men, more than women, are in constant contact with non-
Jews and opportunities for intermarriage are accordingly high. To review these factors must suffice at this point

because their relative importance cannot be ascertained from the available data.

When Jews in Canada intermarry with non-Jews, to what extent do they intermarry with persons of various Christian and other denominations? In Tables IV and V will be found the total number of intermarriages of Jewish men and women with persons of specified religious denominations in each of the quiquennial periods from 1921 to 1960.

The majority of Canadians profess to belong to some non-Catholic Christian denomination, but the largest single Christian denomination in Canada consists of adherents of the Roman Catholic faith. In addition to the Roman Catholics and Greek Catholics there are 22 non-Catholic Christian denominations listed in the Canadian marriage statistics, besides a considerable number who claim to be "Undenominational Christians", without specifying any particular denomination. We have included all those non-Catholic Christian denominations among Protestants. There are also a number of adherents of various Oriental religions, and those who claim to have no religion.

Among the non-Jews with whom the 5,548 Jews who have intermarried in Canada during the period from 1926 to 1960 have associated themselves are 3,746 Protestants, 1,606 Roman Catholics, 98 Greek Catholics, 60 persons professing no religion, 5 members of Oriental religions; 33 persons have left their religious affiliation unspecified. Of the 3,746 Protestants of various denominations, 1,159 were Anglicans or Episcopalians, 1,029 members of the United Church of Canada, 412 Presbyterians, 250 Lutherans, 184 Baptists and 113 members of the Eastern Orthodox Churches. Among the other religions professed by very small numbers of non-Jews who have married Jews during the period from 1926 to 1960 and are listed in

Table IV

Number of Intermarriages among Jewish men in Canada in Quinquennial Periods from 1921 to 1960, classified by religion of non-Jewish brides.

Religion of Non-Jewish Brides.	Total 1921-1960*	1921-1925*	1926-1930	1931-1935	1936-1940	1941-1945	1946-1950	1951-1955	1956-1960
Anglican	850	38	66	41	86	142	166	155	156
United Church	770	30	33	44	75	141	151	155	141
Presbyterian	313	34	26	29	33	47	44	41	59
Lutheran	182	7	16	13	16	25	18	36	51
Baptist	137	6	14	3	16	32	23	20	23
Eastern Orthodox	69	1	1	3	2	7	12	24	19
Christian Science	13	2	2	—	3	2	1	2	1
Mormon	13	—	—	1	3	3	2	4	—
Unitarian	12	—	1	1	—	—	1	1	6
Christ. Disciples	10	—	3	2	—	1	3	1	2
Evangelical	9	1	2	1	1	—	—	1	2
Pentecostal	7	—	—	—	1	—	—	2	2
Salvation Army	7	—	—	2	—	2	2	2	2
Adventist	6	—	1	—	2	2	—	—	1

*Not including the province of Quebec in 1921-26: statistics not available.

Table IV (Continued)

Mennonite	6	—	—	—	—	1	2	1	2
Brethren	2	—	—	—	—	1	1	—	—
Doukhobers	2	—	—	—	—	—	2	—	—
Apostolic Church	1	—	—	—	—	—	1	1	—
Society of Friends	1	—	—	—	—	—	1	—	—
Jehovah's Witnesses	1	—	—	—	—	—	1	—	—
Protestants N.E.S.*	308	7	15	10	35	34	85	64	58
Total Protestants	2,719	126	180	150	273	440	514	512	524
Roman Catholic	1,144	22	63	73	97	172	179	250	288
Greek Catholic	53	—	5	13	4	8	5	13	5
Oriental religions	1	—	—	—	—	—	1	—	—
No religions	32	5	—	1	6	1	7	4	9
Unspecified	25	2	2	—	6	3	5	4	2
Total non-Jewish brides	3,974	155	250	237	386	624	711	783	828
Bride & groom both Jewish	59,878	2,823	6,499	7,284	8,567	8,855	10,144	8,402	7,304
Total Jewish grooms	63,852	2,978	6,749	7,521	8,953	9,479	10,855	9,185	8,132

N.E.S.=Not elsewhere stated.

Table V

Number of Intermarriages among Jewish women in Canada in Quinquennial Periods from 1921 to 1960, classified by religion of non-Jewish grooms.

Religion of Non-Jewish Grooms.	Total 1921-1960*	1921-1925*	1926-1930	1930-1935	1936-1940	1941-1945	1946-1950	1951-1955	1956-1960
Anglican	332	15	19	26	38	66	47	50	71
United Church	302	13	18	24	32	53	58	51	53
Presbyterian	147	14	9	16	19	29	22	21	17
Lutheran	81	6	4	7	6	14	10	14	20
Baptist	56	3	3	1	6	13	6	15	9
Eastern Orthodox	45	2	—	8	4	11	6	6	8
Unitarian	12	—	—	—	—	—	2	5	5
Christian Science	7	—	—	1	1	—	1	3	1
Christ Disciples	7	—	2	2	1	2	—	—	—
Adventist	7	—	—	4	2	—	—	—	1
Mormon	6	1	1	—	1	—	—	—	1
Evangelical	4	—	—	—	—	1	—	2	1
Jehovah's Witnesses	4	—	—	—	—	—	1	1	2

*Not including the province of Quebec in 1921-26: statistics not available.

Table V (Continued)

Mennonite	3	—	—	—	—	—	—	2	1
Spiritualist	2	—	—	—	—	—	2	—	—
Church of Christ	1	—	—	—	1	—	—	—	—
Society of Friends	1	—	—	—	—	1	—	1	—
Protestants, N.E.S.*	191	1	7	10	12	32	46	42	41
Total Protestant	1,208	55	63	99	123	221	202	214	231
Roman Catholic	496	12	20	32	40	81	91	104	116
Greek Catholic	45	—	3	18	6	10	2	2	4
Oriental religions	4	1	—	—	—	1	1	1	—
No religion	38	1	—	3	7	3	5	7	12
Unspecified	8	1	2	1	—	—	—	1	3
Total non-Jewish grooms	1,799	70	88	153	176	316	301	329	366
Bride & groom both Jewish	59,878	2,823	6,499	7,284	8,567	8,855	10,144	8,402	7,304
Total Jewish brides	61,677	2,893	6,587	7,437	8,743	9,171	10,445	8,731	7,670

*N.E.S.=Not elsewhere stated.

Tables IV and V are Unitarians, Christian Scientists, Mormons, Disciples of Christ, Seventh Day Adventists, Mennonites, members of the Salvation Army, members of the Pentecostal Assembly, Jehovah's Witnesses, Doukhobors, and others.

A total of 338 Jews of both sexes, or 2.5 percent of all Jews who married in the quinquennial period of 1926-30 married non-Jews; 1.8 percent married Protestants and 0.7 percent married Catholics. In the period 1956-1960 the number of Jews of both sexes who intermarried in Canada was 1,194, forming 7.6 percent of all who married during that period; 4.8 percent married Protestants, 2.6 percent married Catholics, and 0.2 percent married persons of other denominations or persons who professed no religion.

A total of 250 Jewish men or 3.7 percent of all Jewish men who married during the period 1926-1930 married non-Jews; 2.7 percent married Protestants and 1.0 percent married Catholics. A total of 828 Jewish men, or 10.0 percent of all Jewish men who married during the period 1956-1960 married non-Jews; 6.4 percent married Protestant women and 3.6 percent married Catholic women.

A total of 88 Jewish women, or 1.3 percent of all Jewish women who married during the period from 1926 to 1930 married non-Jewish men; one percent married Protestants and 0.3 percent married Catholics. A total of 366 Jewish women, or 4.8 percent of all Jewish women who married during the period 1956-1960 married non-Jews; 3.0 percent married Protestants, 1.6 percent married Catholics, and 0.2 percent married persons of other religious denominations or those who professed no religion.

In his study on the ethnic origin of the population of Canada[2] the late Professor S.W. Burton Hurd divided the factors affecting intermarriage into calculable and incalculable ones. The calculable factors were length of residence in Canada, percentage of surplus males, and size of religious or ethnic group. Eliminating other factors he concluded that: a) the longer an ethnic group had been in Canada, the greater was the tendency toward intermarriage; b) the larger the surplus of males of marriageable age, the greater was the rate of intermarriage; and c) the larger the percentage a given group forms of the total population, the less was the likelihood of intermarriage. The incalculable factors Professor Burton Hurd listed were largely psychological in character, such as perceived differences in color, social, religious and cultural backgrounds, rural and urban differentials in life-styles, and the like.

On the basis of the calculable factors and by means of a regression equation Hurd worked out a predictable rate of intermarriage which could be compared with the actual rate. He found that this predictable rate of intermarriage among Jews in Canada, based on the calculable factors alone, was a minus quantity in 1921, although the actual rate of intermarriage among Jews in Canada in that year was about 3.4 percent.

Since the surplus of males over females among Jews in Canada as a whole has always been small and was only 28 per thousand in 1951 as compared with 24 per thousand among the total population of all origins, it cannot be considered a decisively contributing factor with regard to the increase in the rate of intermarriage among Jews. However, deviations from this general observation are in evidence in some of the Canadian provinces, as mentioned above.

The ratio of Jews in the total population of Canada was less than one in every thousand prior to 1911, reached a peak of 1.5 percent of the total population in 1931, and fell to 1.4 percent in 1951 and 1961. This low percentage would be a factor working in the direction of a high rate of intermarriage, if it were not for the fact that the majority of the Jews of Canada — over 80 percent — are concentrated in the three large communities of Montreal, Toronto and Winnipeg. As it is, the plus-factor and the minus-factor may well cancel each other out.

Of all Jews living in Canada in 1921 only 40.3 percent were born in Canada, but by 1941 the percentage of the Canadian-born among the Jewish population reached 50.6 percent and by 1951 it had increased to 57.3 percent. The Jewish population of Canada which numbered 170,241 in 1941, absorbed 32,687 additional Jewish immigrants during the period between 1941 and 1961, an increase of 25.6 percent by immigration, as a result of which the percentage of Canadian-born among Canadian Jews decreased slightly to 56.3 percent in 1961. It is probable that in future decades the natural increase, that is, the excess of births over deaths among the Canadian Jewish population will exceed the increase by immigration, as it did during the period from 1921 to 1951. With increased acculturation, the intermarriage rate can be expected to increase substantially above the rate of 8.5 percent recorded in 1960.

The calculable factors affecting intermarriage, according to Hurd, yielded a minus rate of intermarriage among Jews in Canada in 1921. In the meantime, the actual rate of intermarriage among Jews in Canada has increased from 3.4 percent in 1921 to 8.5 percent in 1960 while among the calculable factors only the length of settlement of Jews in Canada has appreciably changed. It must therefore be concluded that the incalculable factors, or rather the factors which do not lend themselves easily to calculation, have changed in such a way that they no longer prevent the substantial and continued rise in the rate of intermarriage among Jews in Canada.

As a matter of fact, Jews in Canada are no longer confined by choice or necessity to specific occupations in which they are remote from daily contact with non-Jews. Even in the manufacture of clothing, in which they used to be dominant a generation ago, they now form a minority amidst an increasing number of French-Canadian, Anglo-Saxon, Polish, Italian and Ukrainian workers, especially female workers.

Further, there is no doubt that in language, education, dress and standard of living, Jews in Canada, whether Canadian-born or immigrants, have become rapidly acculturated to their surroundings. The greater the percentage of Canadian-born among them and the greater the length of residence of the foreign-born in Canada, the looser have become the ties which bind them to traditional forms of Jewish life and association.

While in previous years the more recently arrived immigrant tended to settle at first in areas largely occupied by persons who came from the same country of origin, spoke the same language and followed the same religious faith as he did, this tendency has diminished with the years gone by. Formerly compact areas of Jewish residence have distintegrated as far as their Jewish character is concerned and Jews have spread out to suburban areas where they rarely form a majority of the inhabitants. At any rate, as people have become more mobile and no longer confine themselves in their social or business contacts to those living in the same block or street, residential segregation seems to play a diminished part as a barrier to intermarriage.

Possibly the greatest and, at any rate, the most natural deterrent to intermarriage is a deeper and wider knowledge on the part of Jews of their own religion and traditional culture and an increased attachment to things Jewish. Where this knowledge is diluted until it is barely recognizable and where the attachment becomes perfunctory, intermarriage inevitably will be on the upgrade. On the other hand, a marriage between one who is a Jew merely by accident of birth and who knows little and cares less about anything distinctively Jewish and a non-Jew who knows little and cares less about his own religious background is not really an intermarriage in terms of faith, although it is technically classified as one.

CONCLUSION

The rate of intermarriage among Jews in Canada has increased from 1.9 percent in 1928 to 8.9 percent in 1959 and has become almost the same among Jewish men as among Catholic and Protestant men in the period 1951-1960. It remains more than twice as high among Jewish men than Jewish women. The Jewish intermarriate rate in Canada can be expected to continue to increase in the years to come, especially in view of the fact that no large-scale Jewish immigration is likely to counteract the prevailing trend. Nevertheless, the total intermarriage rate among Jews in Canada remains much lower among Jews than among non-Jews.

The intermarriage rate among Jews is by no means uniform throughout Canada. It is lowest in the province of Quebec, where there is comparatively little social contact between the French speaking Catholic majority, the English speaking Protestant minority, and the still smaller Jewish minority. It is higher in Ontario and Manitoba, and still higher in British Columbia, the prairie provinces and the Atlantic provinces.

The larger a Jewish community and the more developed and fully utilized its religious, educational and recreational facilities, the lower is the rate of intermarriage. Conversely, the smaller and the more isolated a Jewish community is from other and larger Jewish communities, the higher is its rate of intermarriage.

A considerable proportion of the Canadian Jewish community is more recent in its settlement than both the Jewish communities in the United States and in Great Britain. The bonds with the religious traditions and folk-ways of those earlier Jewish settlers who came in the period from 1881 to 1931 are therefore still strong in Canada. But the increase in the rate of out-marriage among Jews indicates that these bonds are weakening and that the Canadian Jewish community is facing the same problems of adaptation as the Jewish communities in the other English speaking countries.

Notes

1. For example: in the year 1960 there were in Canada 1469 Jewish grooms, of whom 1313 married Jewish brides and 156 married non-Jewish brides and 1400 Jewish brides, of whom 1313 married Jewish grooms, and 87 married non-Jewish grooms.

Method "A" would calculate the rate of intermarrias as follows:

Marriages in which both groom and bride were Jewish	1313
Intermarriages-Jewish grooms with non-Jewish brides 156	
Intermarriages-Jewish brides with non-Jewish grooms 87	
Total Jewish Intermarriages	243
Total married couples in which one or both parties were Jewish	1556

Method "B" would calculate the rate of intermarriage as follows:

Total number of Jewish grooms	1469
Total number of Jewish brides	1400
Total number of Jewish grooms and brides	2869
Number of Jewish grooms married to non-Jewish brides 156	
Number of Jewish brides married to non-Jewish grooms 87	
Total number of intermarriages	243

Cf. Louis Rosemberg. "Canada's Jews". p. 100-111. (Montreal, 1939).
    Nathan Goldberg in "The Jewish People-Past and Present". Vol.2.p.29; Dominion Bureau of Statistics, Vital Statistics.
    Annual Report; esp. Canada Yearbook, p. 226 (Ottawa, 1959).

2. S. W. Burton Hurd. "Origin, Birthplace, Nationality and Language of the Canadian People". Dominion Bureau of Statistics. (Ottawa, 1929).

SOME RECENT STUDIES ABOUT
THE EXTENT OF JEWISH OUT-MARRIAGE
IN THE U.S.A.*

by Erich Rosenthal,

In order to measure the extent to which Jewish persons are involved in marriages across religious boundaries, an operational definition of intermarriage is needed. Most students have used the following definition: A person who professes a religion different from that of his spouse is considered to be intermarried. On this basis, persons who have changed their religion prior to marriage in order to conform to the religion of their spouse will not be considered to be involved in an intermarriage. Statistics derived from this definition are considered minimum figures by those students who—with considerable justification—hold that being or becoming a member of a religious group is a matter of deep and complex cultural conditioning which cannot be acquired by a simple change in religious belief. Since a change in one's religious preference can take place prior to as well as any time after marriage, the proportion of intermarried families is subject to change over time.

The extent of intermarriage can be measured in two

different ways, namely through marriage registration data
and through population and community surveys. The latter show the proportion of the religiously mixed households and families to the total population at a given time.
Marriage registration data indicate the rate of mixture
over time.

As the available statistical studies will be reviewed the
reader should keep in mind the fragmentary and uneven
quality of the data. With the exception of Iowa and Indiana, the departments of vital statistics of no state have
collected information on religious preference of bride or
groom. Since surveys of local Jewish communities are designed to strengthen Jewish cultural and communal services, the complete enumeration of mixed households is not
a primary goal of such surveys. It is a by-product, at best.

The data presented below support the sociological law
that intermarriage increases with a lowering of social barriers between the Jewish group and other groups. This
correlation is expressed in two specific ways, namely in relation to the country of origin and in relation to the length
of residence in the United States.

The relationship between intermarriage and country of
origin is clearly demonstrated in Table 1 where intermarriage data are presented for New York City for the years
1908 and 1912. It will be seen that Jewish persons born
in central and western Europe are much more likely to intermarry than persons whose country of origin was located
in eastern and south-eastern Europe. Persons born in Ru-
mania had the lowest rate while persons born in France
had the highest rate. If Drachsler's data are correct—and
there is no reason to doubt their accuracy within the limits of the method used by him[1]—we learn here that, at least
for the Jewish group, barriers existing in the *country of
origin* appear to be most significant. Since it is usually young
adults who enter into marriage, the barriers set up for

TABLE 1

Intermarriage Rates of Jewish Persons by Country of
Origin, New York City, 1908-12*

Country of Origin	Per Cent
Rumania	0.45
Russia	0.62
Turkey	0.80
Austria	0.99
Hungary	2.44
England	3.47
Holland	4.00
United States	4.26
Germany	5.16
France	6.54

*Source: Julius Drachsler, *Democracy and Assimilation*
(New York: 1920) p. 121 (Quoted in Arthur
Ruppin, *Soziologie der Juden* (Berlin: 1930) vol.
I, p. 216).

young people by the conditions of their upbringing appear to be the factor responsible for the extent of intermarriage. Table I also indicates that young people born
in the United States have a tendency toward a relatively
high level of intermarriage.

This latter tendency is explored in greater detail in Table 2. It will be observed that Russian-born Jewish persons (members of the first or immigrant generation) hardly entered into intermarriage at all. However, members of
the second generation (native-born persons of Russian
parentage) had an intermarriage rate of over 3 per cent,
approaching the level of intermarriage of first generation

TABLE 2

Intermarriage Rates of Jewish Persons by Generation
and by Country of Origin, New York City,
1908-12*

Per cent of Jewish Persons Entering Mixed Marriage

A. Russian Jews		B. German Jews	
First (Immigrant) Generation			
Men	Women	Men	Women
0.26	0.47	4.83	2.62
Second Generation			
3.76	3.14	8.85	2.96

*Source: See footnote to Table 1.

German Jews. Tempting as it may be to generalize, from this single observation one cannot conclude that the level of assimilation of the Russian Jews lags one generation behind that of the German Jews. However, there is one bit of evidence—very slim and unrepresentative to be sure—that the rate of Jewish intermarriage has increased considerably since 1912. An analysis of the marriage registration data for the state of Iowa for the year 1953 reveals that 31 per cent of all marriage certificates involving Jews were issued to mixed couples.[2] In citing this statistic it should be kept in mind, that the density and residence pattern of the Jewish population in Iowa is not representative of the patterns prevalent in our northern industrial cities where the large majority of the Jewish population resides.[3]

In the late thirties a number of Jewish communities conducted demographic surveys designed to gather information on the size of the Jewish population as well as on social and personal characteristics of that population. A summary of these surveys was published by the Conference on Jewish Relations.[4] However, with the exception of Trenton, N.J. and San Francisco, Cal., the summaries do not include information on the extent of mixed marriage or on the problem of collecting such information. However, the data from these and other surveys were assembled by Nathan Goldberg and are presented in Table 3. It will be seen that the proportion of intermarried couples ranges from 1.4 per cent in Trenton to 15.1 per cent in Duluth. In three of the six communities the percentage of

TABLE 3

Intermarriage in 1938-39* in Selected American Cities

Year	City	All	Couples Both Jewish	Mixed No.	%
1939	Dallas, Texas	198	186	12	6.1
1939	Duluth, Minn.	385	327	58	15.1
1938	New London, Conn.	517	490	27	5.2
1938	San Francisco, Cal.	10,110	9,412	698	6.9
1938	Stamford, Conn.	882	823	59	6.7
1939	Trenton, N.J.	1,975	1,948	27	1.4

*Based on N. Goldberg, "Jewish Population in the U.S.," *The Jewish People, Past and Present*, vol. II, 1948, p. 29.

intermarried couples was in the neighborhood of 6 per cent. The fact that the results of the various surveys have been assembled in one table should not lead one to the assumption that an identical definition of a Jewish person was applied in all 6 communities or that the enumeration of mixed households was handled in a uniform fashion. In San Francisco, for example, "non-Jewish members of a mixed household were included only if related to either the male or female head and if they expressed no wish to be omitted; all such persons who requested it were omitted from the enumeration."[5] On the basis of this information, we feel justified in inferring that the 1938 survey under-enumerated the mixed households. By contrast, there is some evidence that a survey of San Francisco undertaken in 1959 overestimated the extent of intermarriage. It was found that in 1959, 17.2 per cent of all households were intermarried.[6] In a personal communication the director of the survey indicated that in cases where there was only a formal conversion to Judaism but no positive identification with it, the couple was defined as intermarried. The case of San Francisco serves to highlight the difficulties of measuring a trend, when the operational definitions and practices of enumeration differ from one survey to the next.

Of the other two surveys undertaken in the fifties the findings for Los Angeles reveal the magnitude of intermarriage to be of the same order as was observed in the

TABLE 4

Intermarriage in Selected American Cities
in the 1950's

A.   Los Angeles, Cal., 1953[a].
       The percentage of non-Jews is
       among females   5.8
       among males   1.6

B.   Washington, D.C., 1956[b].
       Total households intermarried: 3,100   11.3

Jewish husbands	2,100	7.8
Jewish wives	1,000	3.5

C. San Francisco, Cal., 1959[c].
     Percentage Intermarried

San Francisco	17.2
Peninsula	20.0
Marin County	37.0

[a]Fred Massarik, *The Jewish Population of Los Angeles,* Los Angeles: Jewish Community Council, 1953.

[b]S. K. Bigman, *The Jewish Population of Greater Washington, in 1956.* (Washington: D.C. The Jewish Community Council of Greater Washington, 1957), p. 125.

[c]Fred Massarik, *The Jewish Population of San Francisco, Marin County and the Peninsula, 1959.* (San Francisco: Jewish Welfare Federation, 1959), p. 44.

thirties. The survey of Greater Washington found that 11.3 per cent of all households were intermarried. Both surveys reveal that it is more common for Jewish men to marry non-Jewish women than for Jewish women to marry non-Jewish men.[6a]

Because of the lack of comparability resulting from a piece-meal approach to the study of the incidence of intermarriage, the results of the 1957 survey undertaken by the U.S. Bureau of the Census are most welcome. This sample survey was aimed, among others, at the enumeration of the religious composition of the American people.[7] The validity of this survey as far as the Jewish population is concerned has been examined by me in detail in a paper entitled, "Five Million American Jews."[8] There I came to the conclusion that prior demographic studies—undertaken by private organizations—are in close agreement with the results of the sample survey undertaken by the Bureau of the Census. Therefore, its findings concerning the extent of intermarriage can be accepted as basically sound and valid.

It should be pointed out that the Census Bureau obtained answers to the question, "What is your Religion?" on a purely *voluntary* basis. It is also worthwhile to emphasize that only 1 per cent of the respondents failed to report on the question of religion. As will be seen from Table 5, the sample survey found that 7.2 per cent of the couples had a non-Jewish partner. The Census Bureau

TABLE 5

Jewish Intermarriage in the United States, 1957*
Married Couples by Religion Reported for the U.S.
Civilian Population, March 1957

Either or both spouses Jewish	1,356,000	100.0
Both Jewish	1,258,000	92.8
One Protestant	57,000	4.2
One Roman Catholic	41,000	3.0

*Source: *Current Population Reports,* Series P-20, No. 79, February 2, 1958

points out that persons who had changed their religion to conform to that of his or her spouse were *not* included in the category of mixed marriage. Altogether, it appears that the Census Bureau considers the recorded percentage of mixed couples a minimum figure. In the words of the Bureau, while "the enumerators were instructed not to assume that all members of a family have the same religion, it is possible that this instruction may have been overlooked in some cases."[9]

The thesis that with increased acculturation, i.e., with a lowering of the social barrier, intermarriage is likely to increase has been empirically verified in a study of the Jewish community of Washington, D.C. It was found that with higher educational and occupational achievement, higher income and greater length of residence in this country—measured in terms of generations—an increase in intermarriage does occur.[10] In view of the fact that it is popularly believed that Jewish education is a deterrent to intermarriage it is interesting to note that Bigman did not find a consistent inverse relationship between Jewish education and intermarriage. My own research, chiefly in Chicago, has led to the finding that the Jewish population believes that a modicum of Jewish education is one part of a three-part device designed to forestall large-scale intermarriage. The other two parts believed to be deterrents are voluntary residential segregation and residence in a high status area.[11] To the best of my knowledge no empirical study has been undertaken to determine whether there is any factual basis to support this apparently widely held belief.

*This paper is a summary of the lecture presented at the Conference.

1. Julius Drachsler, *Intermarriage in New York City*, Studies in History, Economics and Public Law, No. 213, Columbia University, 1921, ch. II.

2. L. E. Chancellor and T. P. Monahan, "Religious Preference and Intermarriage and Divorces in Iowa," *American Journal of Sociology,* LXI (November, 1955) 235.

3. Erich Rosenthal, "Five Million American Jews," *Commentary* XXVI (December, 1958), 501-2.

4. Sophia M. Robison, editor, *Jewish Population Studies* (New York: Conference on Jewish Relations, 1943).

5. Samuel Moment, "A Study of San Francisco Jewry, 1938," in Robison, *op. cit.*, 161.

6. Fred Massarik, *The Jewish Population of San Francisco, Marin County and the Peninsula, 1959* (San Francisco: Jewish Welfare Federation, November, 1959), 44.

6a. It must be emphasized that the figures for the three communities are not comparable inasmuch as the Los Angeles survey reports individuals while the Washington, D.C., survey reports households. Although the San Francisco survey does not specify it, the best inference is that the data relate to married couples.

7. U. S. Bureau of the Census, "Religion Reported by the Civilian Population of the United States: March, 1957," *Current Population Reports*, Series P-20, No. 79, February 2, 1958.

8. Rosenthal, "Five Million American Jews," 500-502. For an analysis of the survey for the three major religious groups see Paul C. Glick, "Intermarriage and Fertility Patterns Among Persons in Major Religious Groups," *Eugenics Quarterly* VII (March, 1960), 31-38.

9. U. S. Bureau of the Census, *op. cit.*, p. 2.

10. Stanley K. Bigman, *The Jewish Population of Greater Washington in 1956* (Washington, D.C.: Jewish Community Council, 1957), 131-33. For an exploratory study of cultural barriers on intermarriage see Jerold S. Heiss, Premarital Characteristics of the Intermarried," *American Sociological Review*, XXV (February, 1960), 47-55.

11. Erich Rosenthal, "Acculturation Without Assimilation? The Jewish Community of Chicago, Illinois," *American Journal of Sociology* LXVI (November, 1960), 287.

INTERMARRIAGE: A SURVEY
OF UNRESEARCHED PROBLEMS

By Joseph Maier

I may not be far wrong in assuming that so much has already been said in this Conference about the urgent problems which call for further research that a detailed listing of "unresearched problems" and a discussion of possible studies seem hardly necessary. In this field, as in many others, the sociologist and the social administrator are not plagued by any lack of important hypotheses. The difficulty is rather that of deciding among multiple possibilities. Yet there may be some value in giving a few illustrations of the types of studies which might be undertaken to test some of the more fruitful hypotheses in this area. I will not try to specify a complete study design in each case. Such an attempt would not be practicable. It would also be self-defeating. Worthwhile research is nothing routine. It is a flexible and inventive process responsive to specific times and circumstances. Any concrete designs outlined in advance are likely to be out of date or inappropriate in the time and place in which one may eventually have an opportunity to apply them. Accordingly, I shall simply list and appraise a limited number of diversified projects as representative of a much larger and more systematic range of fruitful studies which might be undertaken in this field.

Such studies as I have in mind may conveniently be grouped as seeking answers to three principal types of questions: (1) What is the size and scope of Jewish-Gentile intermarriage in the United States? (2) What are the decisive variables determining the rate of such intermarriages? (3) What is the outcome of such intermarriages? Let me discuss them *seriatim.*

I

There is a curious discrepancy between the concern and agitation of many American Jews over the growing number of intermarriages which they regard as a serious threat to the survival of the Jewish group in this country on the one hand, and the reassuring findings of social scientists that the number of Jewish-Gentile intermarriages has always been small on the other. What is the size of the problem? More specifically, how many American Jews marry outside their faith? To this elementary question we can give only the haziest answer. The Federal Census includes no questions about ancestry or religious affiliation. What we know, we have been forced to infer from polls and community studies of limited quantity and varying quality. Neither opinion nor community studies to date have been such as to permit estimates of the incidence of Jewish-Gentile intermarriage to be made with any degree of reliability. To put it bluntly: Whether you receive a "reassuring" or "discouraging" answer to the question, "How many Jews marry outside their faith?", depends on what studies you select.

To be sure, most studies of Jewish intermarriage in the United States report low percentages. In her famous

New Haven studies, Ruby Kennedy[2] found that approximately 5 per cent of the Jewish marriages were interfaith, and Hollingshead[3] discovered that 91 per cent of *all* marriages involved partners from the same religious group. In the case of the Jews, this percentage was 97.1, among the Catholics it was 93.8. It fell to 74.4 per cent for Protestants. The differences in percentage, Hollingshead believes, are a reflection of the relative intensity of in-group sanctions in the three religious groups. In other words, he found that Jewish group efforts to maintain control in mate selection have been more effective than either Catholic or Protestant.

A striking point that emerged from both the Kennedy and Hollingshead data is that the effects of religion on marital choice have not changed between the parental and the present generation. The number of Catholics who married Catholics and of Jews who married Jews, was almost the same in both generations. The number of Protestants who married Protestants dropped in the present generation, but not significantly in terms of the numbers involved.[4] The influence of religious affiliation in the selection of a marriage partner, Hollingshead concludes, is obviously strongest in the Jewish group and weakest in the Protestant, a fact he found reflected in the number of mixed marriages.

The same picture emerges from studies made in New York, Cincinnati, and Stamford. The very low incidence of intermarriage may also be inferred from a recent study of Jewish population shifts towards suburbia in the Chicago area by Erich Rosenthal.[5] The recent aggregation of the Jewish community on the northside of Chicago and its northern suburbs is explained as the result of the discriminatory features of the housing market as well as the desire of many Jews for "voluntary segregation." Voluntary segregation in a high-status area, indeed, appears to be effective in inhibiting large-scale intermarriage. To put it somewhat differently: The one thing Jewish parents seem to fear more than anything else, and fear today more than at any other time in history, is amalgamation or, more precisely, what they consider the decisive step thereto, namely the out-marriage of their children. In order to forestall such an event, the parents favor residence in a neighborhood that has such a high density of Jewish families that the statistical probability of their children marrying a Jewish partner approaches certainty.

If this is true, regardless whether such voluntary segregation will prove to be a universally effective or desirable "survival formula," if religion is really so strong a control in the selection of marriage mates as these studies would make it appear, why the deep concern with the problem of intermarriage?

It may, of course, be that the above studies do not provide an accurate gauge of the scope of the problem, or that they tell only part of the story. Let us, therefore, look at another set of studies. A number of private communal surveys conducted in the 1930's revealed that no more than roughly 6 per cent of Jewish families in this country were intermarried.[6] Even a first official report on the religious composition of the American people indicated that in 1957 only 7.2 per cent of all Jewish families had a non-Jewish marriage partner.[7] However, recent reports also revealed that in New York City Jews intermarry at a rate of 18.4 per cent[8]; in Washington, D.C. at the rate of 11.5 per cent[9]; in Iowa at the rate of 31 per cent[10]; in San Francisco at the rate of 17.2 per cent, on the peninsula and in Marin County at the rates of 20 per cent and 37 per cent respectively.[11]

Where does this leave us with regard to the question of the number of Jews intermarrying in the United States? Clearly, the answer turns on your assumptions. As Rosenthal puts it,[12] if we accept the findings of the 1957 *Current Population Reports* of a national intermarriage rate of 7.2 per cent, and if, at the same time, we assume that the statistics for Iowa and the San Francisco area are merely regional variations of the over-all rate, we may be justified in saying there is no rapidly growing threat to Jewish group survival through intermarriage. If we assume, however, that the findings for Iowa and the San Francisco area are the first indications of the future overall rate of intermarriage, then Jewish group survival becomes rather doubtful.

We are thus left with the realization that, as we have no complete and continuing statistics for the United States as a whole, we have no sure way of determining the size of the problem. Which is another way of saying that neither the fears nor the hopes regarding the incidence of intermarriage can be adequately justified by the figures available to us at this time. We may be reasonably certain, however, that both Catholics and Protestants marry and will continue to marry across religious lines much more frequently than do Jews.

II

Assuming for the moment that we knew what we don't know, namely how many Jews marry non-Jews in the United States, we would still wish to know the answer to our second type of question: What factors determine the interfaith marriage rate? In what social context do intermarriages occur? Are they more common among professionals, businessmen or trade union members? Among people living in the large metropolitan centers, small towns or suburbs?

Students of marriage have formulated two responses to the question of who marries whom. In the main, they have held (a) that birds of a feather flock together and/or (b) that opposites attract each other. While psychologists have confined their attention chiefly to individual physical and psychological characteristics and stressed that mate selection tends to operate on the basis of complementary needs,[13] sociologists have emphasized that mate selection is generally homogamous with respect to race, ethnicity, social class, residential propinquity and, of course, religion. Which amounts to saying that generally a Jew, for example, will marry a Jew in accordance with the rules of his religion and that, moreover, he is more or less compelled by his culture to marry a Jew of the same or similar social status, race, and neighborhood, although he has a choice as to the precise individual.

In considering the social conditions that favor interfaith marriages, let us focus, first, on the factor of propinquity. A number of studies have been made in recent decades of the effects of residential propinquity on mate selection. The results may be fairly summed up in the statement, "Cupid may have wings, but he does not fly very far."[14] Koller who applied even "more rigorous techniques" than previous investigators to determine the validity of residential propinquity as a factor of mate selection, concluded confidently that "here we might have a device of great predictive value."[15] It would, hence, seem reasonable to assume that when one religious group has few representatives in a community, many out-marriages will occur. Indeed, Thomas[16] has found that rates of Catholic-Protestant marriages are high in areas where there is a low proportion of Catholics in the population, thus reducing the number of persons from which individual selection of a spouse of the same faith can be made.

How about marriages between Jews and non-Jews? Is the same pattern discernible in their case? In describing the vigilance of Jewish parents regarding friendships between boys and girls which might lead to dating and court-

ship and subsequently to love and marriage, Barron has
this to say about the situation in a Connecticut town of
10,000:

> "Although it is quite common for a Jewish boy in
> Derby to have friends of his own sex among Gentiles, it
> is only rarely that he will have a Gentile "girl friend."
> One or two dates of this sort are sufficient for the rela-
> tionship to become a topic of gossip in the community.
> In such cares, word usually reaches Jewish parents quite
> rapidly and they plead with their wayward sons to "stop
> bothering with *Shikses* because there are plenty of fine
> Jewish girls in town." More or less the same is true of
> Jewish girls. In fact, it is even more difficult for them
> than for unmarried Jewish males to cross the religious
> line hetero-sexually. The male friends of Jewish girls
> are very carefully checked, more so than in the case of
> Gentile girls."[17]

In any case, Barron believes that one significant factor
in the low rate of intermarriage of Derby Jews is that the
young people of this town have contacts with the larger
Jewish communities in nearby New Haven and Bridge-
port. The area of choice is thus greatly widened so that
someone of compatible personality as well as Jewish religion is more likely to be found than if the selection of the
spouse were limited to the smaller community.[18]

If marriages between Jews and non-Jews are both low
and high in the metropolitan centers, in the small towns
and in the suburbs, where, then, are they either high or
low? Do intermarriages occur at random? Highly unlikely.
But the evidence thus far permits of no clear answer. Perhaps residential propinquity is not an essential variable.
Perhaps it applies only to non-mobile groups. It may be a
factor easily subsumable to quantitative breakdown, but
"does not by itself explain mate selection any more than
geographical factors by themselves definitely explain dif-

ferences in social and cultural life among different peoples."[19] Anyhow, I know of Jewish communities in some New Jersey suburbs with an out-marriage rate as high as 15 per cent among *temple members*—and this with the largest Jewish hinterland in the world, New York City, to rely on for social contacts.

Now consider socio-economic status. We have studies to show that Catholics outmarry more frequently in upper social classes than in lower, as measured by rental areas in one city. Among 51,671 families in one large city the percentages of families living in different areas that were based on mixed marriages increased regularly from 8.5 per cent in the lowest rental area to 17.9 per cent in the highest, with 19.3 per cent among suburban families.[20] Although the study in question did not venture an explanation, it is likely that persons in the higher rental areas were also those with less ethnic affiliation and with higher education. "Both of these factors would tend to increase their contacts in both number and variety with persons of other religious faiths and to free them from strict compliance with religious rules."[21]

What of the out-marriages of Jews? Do they also occur more frequently in the upper classes? We don't really know. To be sure, the recent survey of the Jewish population of Washington, D.C. was detailed enough to show that American-born Jews with an educational achievement beyond high school and high professional status are most likely to out-marry.[22] We ought to examine what the situation is like in the New York needle trades before we generalize. On the other hand, to the extent that American Jews have by and large become members of the middle class and the upper-middle class, that is, to the degree that they already possess high socio-economic status, what incentive is there for them to move out of their class at all? How much higher than high can you get? It is obvious that we must await the results of further research before we can properly assess the significance of the SES (=Socio-Economic Status) variable in Jewish-Gentile intermarriages.

A word about ethnicity may be in order. Ethnicity is closely allied with religion, perhaps especially so in the case of the Jews. While the coincidence of religion and ethnicity tends to reduce out-marriages, it must be agreed that marriages across ethnic lines are more frequent today. According to the New Haven studies mentioned earlier, cross-ethnic marriages occur more frequently in the present than in the parent generation within both the Catholic and the Protestant religions. This is said not to hold true for the Jews. Kennedy, for example, found that in 1870 in-marriage among Jews was 100 per cent. It has been rightly observed[23] that Kennedy here takes Jewishness as an ethnic variable, which it is not. Nor does she distinguish between West and East European Jews. In 1870 they were probably mainly of German, later mainly of Russian and Polish origin. But whatever the particular situation in New Haven, ethnic differences did sunder western from eastern Jews to the extent that marriage between them was frowned upon. The same was true of the relations between *Litvaks* and *Galizianer*.

The sundering characteristics of ethnicity, however, are wearing thin. Second and third generation Jews speak American without a European accent. Which brings to mind the question: What happened to the Sephardic and German-Bohemian Jews who used to be, but are no longer prominent in American Jewish life? There are some who believe they were more prone than others to marry across religious lines and eventually dissolved in the melting pot. There are some who believe that the same fate awaits American Jewry generally as it becomes more American with each new generation. German Jews have become amalgamated all right, but it is my impression that they have fused chiefly with Jews of East European origin. In other words, there is good reason to hypothesize that inter-marriage patterns tend to be endogamous in religion and class, but exogamous ethnically.[24] Also, it has been ob-served that the older and better established groups tend to limit outmarriage beyond the third generation and to re-turn to a homogamous marriage pattern.[25]

Sociologists recognize that indoctrination from child-hood in any of the religious cultures means more than a difference in theological beliefs. But very little research has to date been undertaken about the early patterns of interaction. We certainly need to know more about what situations in the family predispose people to outmarry or make it possible for them to overcome the usual barriers to outmarriage. Jerold Heiss has recently addressed him-self to this important question in an exploratory report on the premarital characteristics of the religiously intermar-ried.[26] His study was based on data from the New York Midtown Mental Health Project. His sample consisted of 304 outmarried and 863 inmarried respondents from the midtown area in Manhattan. If categories are combined, Heiss notes, Catholics have an outmarriage rate of 21.4 per cent, and Jews one of 18.4, both considerably lower than the Protestant rate of 33.9, with the incidence of Jewish-Catholic marriages about equal to that of Jewish-Protestant unions. What regularities did Heiss discover as the situa-tions facilitating the removal of barriers to outmarriage?

He found that, in general, the outmarried as compared with the inmarried are characterized by (a) non-religious parents, (b) greater dissatisfaction with parents when young, (c) greater amount of early family strife, (d) less early family integration, and (e) greater emancipation from parents at time of marriage. Specifically, the Catholic data bear out these five hypotheses. In the Protestant group, only two of the general hypotheses receive substantial support, that is, outmarried Protestants had relatively weak ties to family and religion. But, significantly again, to the Jewish group none of the hypotheses were found to apply, save perhaps one: the outmarried were more likely to report tenuous ties to immediate and extended family when young.[27]

Surely, it appears that close ties to immediate and extended family when young augur well for inmarriage. In other words, if observant grandparents are around, chances are relatively good that there will be no outmarriage. But how well do close relations with extended family go with living in a democratic industrial society? Parsons has argued that extended family relations are antithetical to democratic industrial societies because they are not consonant with occupational mobility.[28] Or can it be said that inmarried Jews provide a good example of the hypothesis that a "modified" extended family is consonant with occupational mobility in the mature industrial economy?[29] Clearly, much additional work remains to be done in this area.

To pass on to another matter deserving attention under this rubric, Hollingshead found that there is no consistent bias as between sex and mixed Catholic-Protestant marriages, with either partner likely to be a Catholic or a Protestant. In Jewish-Gentile marriages, on the other hand, he found that it has been a Jewish male who married a Gentile female.[30] That the Jewish man is much more likely to outmarry than is the Jewish woman, has been confirmed by other studies. Baber found in a study of 130 intermarriages in New York City that Jewish men outmarry about twice as frequently as do Jewish women,[31] and Barron discovered that in 59 intermarriages the Jewish partner was male in 40 cases.[32] In an attitude study of 3,000 students, Landis found that the Jewish men were much more willing to marry outside their faith than the

women, but if the women also said they would marry outside their faith more than a third said they would change
their faith to that of the spouse; conversely, only 12 per
cent of the men said they would change their faith.[33]

If there is a greater tendency for the Jewish man to out-
marry—and I am not wholly satisfied that this is the case—
it is hardly sufficient to explain this on the basis of the
closer parental supervision of the girls' dating activities
and the greater freedoms allowed to the boys. Were this
the case, it would apply to American boys and girls generally, not only to those of the Jewish faith. It may be, of
course, that Jewish parents tend to scrutinize their daughters' boy friends more rigorously than Gentile parents, and
while they may try to do the same for their sons, they fail
because of the wider mobility generally accorded to men
as a prerogative of their sex. Simpson believes that, since
many of the outmarried Jews in the above studies had parents who were foreign born or ethnically close to the Old
World, "there may be at work here an involved Oedipus
situation in which these Jewish men revolt against the emotional dominion of their fathers, a revolt catapulted into
social action by the desire to be accepted by the out-group
who stand as a revolt symbol against the foreign-born father."[34] How is the lesser tendency of Jewish females toward outmarriage to be accounted for? Very simply: Jewish women, like all women, are somewhat less oedipally
rebellious. What of the outmarried Jews who are neither
foreign born nor ethnically close to the Old World? Further, may we expect that as American Jews become increasingly native and the distinguishing marks of ethnicity
wear away, the Oedipus situation will no longer express
itself in outmarriaage? Simpson does not say, but he mentions the possibility that involved here also is a Jewish sex
ratio which is adverse to Jewish men in some geographical
areas. That possibility is hard to deny, indeed.

III.

We now come to the third type of unresolved questions about Jewish-Gentile marriages: What is their outcome?

Here, a host of specific questions come to mind which need to be researched very badly. How many persons among the intermarried convert to Judaism and how many out of Judaism? Who are they? Males or females? Are they of high SES or those of low SES? Urban, suburban or rural? How many of the outmarried who are religiously alienated remain socially and culturally Jews? How many socialize predominantly with other intermarried couples? How many children do the intermarried have and what happens to them religiously and culturally? Further, how many of the children in this particular group remarry into Judaism culturally and/or religiously, and why? How happy are the intermarried, those with and those without children? Again, who are they?

The consequences of interfaith marriages have not been thoroughly studied. This is true of interreligious marriages in general and Jewish-Gentile marriages in particular. The relevant research literature seems to confirm, with notable exceptions, the popular belief that interfaith marriages are less stable than intrafaith marriages. Exactly *why* this should be so, is not clearly established, however.

One of the more significant efforts in this field was made in 1949 by Landis who used his students at Michigan State College and their parents as his sample. What did he find regarding the effects of religious differences on marital stability? From an analysis of his sample of 4,108 marriages, he concluded: "Approximately 5 per cent of the Catholic and Jewish marriages ended in divorce or separation, 8 per cent of the Protestant marriages, 15 per cent of the mixed Catholic-Protestant, and 18 per cent of the marriages in which there was no religious faith"[35]. Two things seem to be characteristic of this study as well as of most other studies: (1) While it indicates that interfaith marriage is seemingly more hazardous than intrafaith marriages, even the interfaith marriages are reported to be overwhelmingly stable. (2) The study contains no data about Jewish-Gentile intermarriages.

Do children affect family adjustment? Decidedly so, says Landis. "In fact, the results of our study among couples with children would lead us to believe that if there are no children, the Catholic-Protestant marriage has few elements which would make marital adjustment difficult."[36] Would that hold true for Jewish-Gentile marriages as well? We do not know.

What happens to the children of mixed marriages? Baber found that the children of Jewish-Catholic marriages and Jewish-Protestant marriages were brought up in the Jewish religion more frequently than in either the Catholic or the Protestant religion.[37] Does this indicate that in Jewish-Gentile marriages the Jewish parent prevails in the religious training of the child? Or does it mean that the father generally prevails, on the assumption that in such marriages the Jewish partner is more often the husband?

On the other hand, the Landis study mentioned above shows that the children of mixed marriages were reared in the mother's faith from 2 to 3 times as often as in the father's faith, regardless whether the mother was Catholic or Protestant. While, as we noted, Landis found too few Jewish-Gentile marriages to make possible a similar comparison for them, his finding is in accord with my own information about some Jewish communities in New Jersey suburbs, where most of the 15 per cent outmarried among Temple members are Jewish women who are eager to send their children to Temples' religious schools. Apart from the fact that from a strictly *halachic* (religio-legal) point of view the children of Jewish mothers are Jews, there

are other reasons why we think that the religion of
the mother is more likely to be followed by the children
than that of the father. It is generally agreed that the middle class mother takes more responsibility for rearing the
children than does the father.

On the other hand, parents often solve the dilemma by
acquainting their children with both religions and letting
them choose for themselves, either Hanukka or Christmas,
either the Menorah or the Christmas tree, or both, or neither. But what is the general pattern? Again, we don't
know. We do not know enough about the salient variables
to make any reasonable generalizations. We know only individual cases.

What of family resistance to accepting the member of
the outgroup? Slotkin[38] in his study of 183 Jewish-Gentile
intermarriages found that 57 per cent of the intermarried
were either partially or wholly accepted by both families;
20 per cent of the Jews were not accepted by their own
families, and 23 per cent were not accepted by the family
of the Gentile spouse; 16 per cent of the Gentiles were not
accepted by their own families, and 27 per cent were not
accepted by the spouse's family. It appears from this study
that, if there is to be rejection, Jewish families are more
likely to do the rejecting than non-Jewish families. Here
again, there is need to inquire further into the why's and
wherefore's and the validity of samples.

There are other problems which deserve careful study
and clarification. Take, for example, the confusing problem of terminology, to which, I am afraid, I may have
added. Most of the time, we use the terms "intermarriage"
and "mixed marriage" interchangeably. But rarely, if ever,
is it made clear in either the literature or in colloquial
usage that if we refer to a marriage between a Jew and a
Gentile who has been converted to Judaism as an intermarriage or mixed marriage, we are making a *historical,*

not a present, statement.[39] Or take the question of possible differences in outcome between Protestant-Jewish and Catholic-Jewish marriages. Baber[40] seems to think that the best prognosis for an interfaith marriage is to be expected between Protestant and Jew, the poorest between Catholic and Protestant—the latter being a slightly greater risk than that between Catholic and Jew. May be so. We don't really know. We may, of course, freely speculate about this and other questions raised here, but we must also realize that all hypotheses are of little value without the data necessary to validate them.

There is also a more fundamental task confronting us as sociologists. As Barron put it, we must call attention to the inconsistency of conservative attitudes toward intermarriage on the one hand with activities in creating social and cultural conditions favoring intermarriage on the other hand. Sending children to public schools and to centers of higher education away from home, struggling against restrictive covenants, job discrimination, and quota systems, participating in interfaith activity, are but a few representative practices which lead inevitably to intergroup contacts and subsequently to love and marriage. The recognition of this dilemma is fundamental to any intelligent approach to the problem.

Once we have the data, we may yet find that intermarriage, while indicating the lessening of some social controls, need not end in disaster to the personality, the marriage, or the group. We may find that intermarriage is not the crucial index of the amalgamative process, that adjustments can be made and are made much more frequently than we are now inclined to believe, and that, far from facing extinction, a new growth is in store for the Jewish community in the United States.

What we will find, I do not pretend to know. But there is nothing in the facts or the logic of the situation to prevent work of great practical importance from being done in the years now before us. Neither marriage nor intermarriage occurs at random. Both occur in accordance with discernible patterns, and the design for valuable research in this field does not in principle differ from that in any other field. Given the determination to undertake such studies, and given the requisite funds for that purpose, advances of the first order may be achieved.

1. Cf. M. L. Barron, "The Incidence of Jewish Intermarriage in Europe and America," *American Sociological Review*, 11 (February 1946), 7.

2. Ruby Jo Reeves Kennedy, "Single or Triple Melting Pot? Intermarriage Trends in New Haven, 1870-1950", *American Journal of Sociology*, 5 (July 1952), 56.

3. August B. Hollingshead, "Cultural Factors in the Selection of Marriage Mates," *American Sociological Review*, 15 (1950), 619-27.

4. Cf. Simon Marcson, "Intermarriage and Generational Status", *Phylon*, 4 (1951), 457-63.

5. Erich Rosenthal, "Acculturation without Assimilation? The Jewish Community of Chicago, Illinois", *American Journal of Sociology*, 66 (November 1960), 275-88.

6. Nathan Goldberg, "Jewish Population in the United States", *The Jewish People Past and Present*, II (New York: Jewish Encyclopedic Handbooks, 1948), 29.

7. "Religion Reported by the Civilian Population of the United States, March 1957", *Current Population Reports*, Series P-20, No. 79 (Washington, D.C., February 2, 1958), p. 125.

8. Jerold S. Heiss, "Premarital Characteristics of the Religiously Intermarried in an Urban Area", *American Sociological Review*, 25 (February 1960), 47-55.

9. Stanley K. Bigman, *The Jewish Population of Greater Washington in 1956* (Washington, D.C.: Jewish Community Council, May 1957), 125.

10. Loren E. Chancellor and Thomas P. Monahan, "Religious Preference and Interreligious Mixtures in Marriages and Divorces in Iowa", *American Journal of Sociology*, 61 (November 1955), 235.

11. Fred Massarik, *The Jewish Population of San Francisco, Marin County and the Peninsula, 1959* (San Francisco: Jewish Welfare Federation, November 1959), 44.

12. Erich Rosenthal, *op. cit.*, 228.

13. Cf. Robert F. Winch, *The Modern Family* (New York: Henry

Holt & Co., 1952), pp. 391-433. Also Thomas and Virginia Ktsanes, "The Theory of Complementary Needs in Mate Selection", in: Robert F. Winch and Robert McGinnis (eds.), *Selected Studies in Marriage and the Family* (New York: Henry Holt & Co., 1953), 435-53.

14. J. H. S. Bossard, *Marriage and Family* (Philadelphia: University of Pennsylvania Press, 1940), 79-92.

15. Marvin R. Koller, "Residential and Occupational Propinquity", in: Robert F. Winch and Robert McGinnis (eds.), *Op. cit.*, 434.

16. John L. Thomas, "The Factor of Religion in the Selection of Marriage Mates", *American Sociological Review*, 16 (August 1951), 489.

17. Milton L. Barron, *op. cit.*, 8.

18. *Ibid.*

19. George Simpson, *People in Families* (New York: Thomas Y. Crowell Co., 1960), 131-32.

20. John L. Thomas, *op. cit.*, 490.

21. Ruth Shonle Cavan, *The American Family* (New York: Thomas Y. Crowell Co., 1953), p. 251.

22. Stanley K. Bigman, *op. cit.*, pp. 131-33.

23. George Simpson, *op. cit.*, 138-39.

24. Simon Marcson, "A Theory of Intermarriage and Assimilation," *Social Forces*, 29 (October 1950), 75-8.

25. Simon Marcson, "Intermarriage and Generational Status", *loc. cit.*

26. Jerold S. Heiss, *op. cit.*

27. *Ibid.*, 53-4.

28. Talcott Parsons, "Revised Analytical Approach to the Theory of Social Stratification", in: R. Bendix and S. M. Lipset (eds), *Class, Status and Power* (Glencoe, Ill.: Free Press, 1953), 116 et sequ.

29. Cf. Eugene Litwak, "Occupational Mobility and Extended Family Cohesion", *American Sociological Review*, 25 (February 1960), 9-21.

30. Hollingshead, *op. cit.*

31. Ray E. Baber, *Marriage and the Family* (New York: McGraw Hill Book Co., 1953), 102.

32. Barron, *op. cit.*, 12.

33. Judson T. Landis, "Marriages of Mixed and Non-Mixed Religious Faith", *American Sociological Review*, 14 (1949), 401-7.

34. George Simpson, *op. cit.*, 136.

35. Landis, *op. cit.*

36. *Ibid.*

37. Baber, *op. cit.*, 103.

38. J. S. Slotkin, "Adjustment in Jewish-Gentile Intermarriages", *Social Forces*, 21 (December 1942), 226-30.

39. Baber, *op. cit.*, 167-73.

40. Cf. Salomon B. Freehof, "Report on Mixed Marriages and Inter-marriage", *Yearbook*, 57 (Philadelphia: Central Conference of American Rabbis, 1947). Also David Max Eichhorn, "A New Look at Conversion and Marriage", *CCAR Journal* (January 1957), 10-17.

41. M. L. Barron, "Race, Religion, and Nationality in Mate Selection", in: Morris Fishbein and Ruby Jo Reeves Kennedy, (eds.) *Modern Marriage and Family Living* (New York: Oxford University Press, 1957), 72.

SPECIAL CASES

CONVERSION:
REQUIREMENTS AND RESULTS

By David Max Eichhorn

The place of a paper on conversion in a symposium on
intermarriage is contingent upon the following considerations. It is, to begin with, readily admitted that there is
no organic connection between conversion and intermarriage. A non-Jew who converts to Judaism becomes a Jew.
Judaism is a universal, not a racial or national, religion.
Therefore, a marriage between a born Jew and a converted Jew is not an intermarriage. A marriage between
a born Jew and a converted Jew is, in every respect, a Jewish marriage. This strict and narrow view, however, while
technically correct, does not take the whole truth into account. If all Jews had a correct understanding of the teachings of Judaism with regard to converts and conversion,
this paper would be completely out of place in this symposium. Unfortunately, however, the teachings of Judaism do not always fully coincide with the actual beliefs
and feelings of many Jews. The fact is that many Jews are
so ignorant of Jewish teachings about conversion and harbor such deep prejudices towards converts that in

111

their minds, a marriage between a born Jew and a converted Jew is still an intermarriage. This is why this paper fits into this symposium.

The subject of conversion to Judaism is a very large subject. As the title of this paper indicates, I shall discuss here two aspects only of the current conversion situation:

a) The present requirements for conversion to Judaism of the Orthodox, Conservative and Reform groups, and

b) The end-result of this conversion process, that is the quality of the converts as Jews.[1]

Requirements

The Orthodox requirements for conversion are based directly on the provisions of that sixteenth century lawcode known as the *Shulhan Arukh*. The key section of the Shulhan Arukh dealing with this matter is chapter 268 of the *Yore De'ah*. Even in relatively recent editions, this chapter is prefaced by a pathetic and revealing note which informs the reader that its regulations apply only in those places where the civil authorities permit Jews to accept converts.

I shall present verbatim the most pertinent portions of this chapter (the translation is from the 1926 Vilna Hebrew edition):

1. The first requirement for a male proselyte entering the Jewish fold is circumcision (Talmud B. *Yebamot* 46a). Even if he was previously circumcised or if he was born circumcised, it is still necessary to draw a drop of blood of the covenant (Maimonides, *Hilkhot Mila,* chap. 1).

2. When one presents himself as a candidate for conversion, he is asked: "What motivates you? Do you not know that, in these days, Jews are subject to persecution and discrimination, that they are hounded

and troubled?" If he replies: "I know this and yet I regard myself as unworthy of being joined to them," he is accepted immediately (*Yebamot* 47a). The root principles of our faith, i.e., the unity of God and the prohibition of idol-worship, are expounded to him at considerable length (Maim., *Hilkh. Issure Biah,* chap. 14). He is taught, too, some of the simpler and some of the more difficult commandments. This negative aspect is not explained at great length nor in detail. Moreover, just as he is informed of the punishments for violating the commandments, so, too, is he told of the rewards for observing them, particularly that, by virtue of keeping them, he will merit the life in the world to come (*Yebamot* 47a) . . . . He is also told: "Know that the World to Come is intended only for the righteous. When you see Jews in distress in this world, their suffering is in reality future merit stored up for them in the World to Come. Unlike the idolators, Jews do not receive the major portion of their reward here, lest they become puffed up with pride and go astray and lose their eternal reward. Nevertheless, the Holy One, blessed be He, does not overburden the Jews with troubles that might cause them to perish. On the contrary, the idolatrous nations will perish, but Israel will survive." This theme is expounded at considerable length so that the convert may properly appreciate the place of Israel in the Divine scheme (*Yebamot* 47a). After his circumcision is completely healed, he undergoes ritual immersion (*Yebamot* 47b). Three learned Jews stand by, while he is in the water, and instruct him a second time in some of the easy and some of the difficult commandments. In the case of a female proselyte, Jewish women accompany her and immerse her up to her neck. The three learned male Jews remain out-

side the immersion chamber and give the convert instruction while she is in the water (Asheri). After
the immersion, the convert is regarded as a full-
fledged Jew. If he reverts to his former faith, he is
treated as a Jewish apostate. If he marries a Jewess,
the marriage remains valid even after his apostasy
(*Yebamot* 47b).

3. The process involved in preparing a candidate for conversion—instruction, circumcision and immersion—
requires the presence of a legal court of three learned
Jews . . .

6. If a pregnant woman is converted, the child born subsequently requires no immersion (*Yebamot* 78a).

7. A minor may be converted if his father gives consent.
If he has no father and comes of his own accord or is
brought by his mother, a Jewish court may convert
him, because becoming Jewish is beneficial and it is
permissible to confer a benefit on a minor without his
consent. However, any minor so converted may, if he
so desires, renounce the conversion after he attains
maturity. Such a relapsed person is not considered an
apostate but simply reassumes the status of a non-Jew
(B. Talmud *Ketubot* 11a).

8. The ruling just cited applies to one who, after coming of age, does not live as an observant Jew. One
who lives as an observant Jew after coming of age is
not permitted to nullify his conversion (*Ketubot*
11a) . . . .

10. Non-Jews who are observed over a period of time to
be living as faithful Jews and to be keeping all the
commandments, are regarded as converts, even
though there be no witnesses to prove that they were
ever formally converted. Nevertheless, if such an observant person wishes to marry a Jew, he must either
bring positive proof of conversion or undergo ritual

immersion for the specific purpose of conversion. There is also a strong opinion that one who comes and states that he is a non-Jew who has been converted properly, is to be believed. Maimonides explains that, in an environment where the Jews are in the majority, the non-Jew who claims to be a convert is to be believed, but in an environment where the Jews are in the minority, the non-Jew is not to be allowed to marry a Jewess unless he brings proof of conversion, because, in the latter instance, he is transferring from a less to a more favorable moral environment.

11. One who has been living for a long time in the Jewish community and who declares: "I was born as a non-Jew and I became a Jew simply by living a Jewish life and I consider both my children and myself to be Jews" is not to be considered a Jew but his children are to be considered Jews.

There are many more interesting references to *Gerut* and *Gerim* in this and other parts of the *Shulhan Arukh* which cannot be mentioned here because of lack of space. However, I have quoted verbatim and at some length from this chapter of Yore De'ah to make one point very clear, i.e., that, in this area of *Gerut,* there are quite a number of contemporary Orthodox rabbis who are inclined to be much more stringent in their attitudes and requirements than are those set forth in the law-code which they claim as their guide, namely, the *Shulhan Arukh.*

Conservative rabbis, as a group, follow quite closely the pattern established in the *Shulhan Arukh.* The average length of time they spend in preparing a candidate for conversion is 4.1 months. In New York City, some converts are prepared by being tutored by students of the Jewish Theological Seminary for a period of three months. The course of study, formulated by the Rabbinical Assembly of America, includes a survey of Jewish history, a mastery of the mechanical reading of Hebrew, a study of Jewish holy days and ceremonies, the differences between Judaism and Christianity, the problems of Jewish living, attendance at all three types of worship (Orthodox, Conservative and Reform) and the required reading of various books on Jewish subjects. The books and discussions are adapted to the mental and cultural levels of the candidates. In Chicago, a similar procedure is followed by the Beth Din Council of the Conservative rabbis of that city. All Conservative rabbis require circumcision for male converts but not all require *mikveh* for either male or female converts. One Conservative rabbi states that he requires mikveh only if the future marriage partner is Orthodox. Another states that he sometimes substitutes a public conversion ceremony in the synagogue for the mikveh requirement.

With regard to conversion, as in so many other matters, Reform rabbis do not adhere to the laws of the Shulhan Arukh. Circumcision is not required of an adult male convert nor is the ritual bath of either a male or a female convert. There is a period of instruction which averages 3.7 months. Schools for candidates for conversion are conducted by the Reform group in a number of cities, including New York, Boston, Chicago and Los Angeles. The New York school operates for five sessions each year. Each session is nine weeks long. The number of students in each session runs from about 25 to 50. The study course consists essentially of instruction in Jewish history, theology, ethics, and customs and ceremonies. Only about one Reform rabbi in twenty requires the convert to have a reading knowledge of Hebrew before conversion. It should be mentioned here that, while the rules of the Rabbinical Assembly require that the Conservative rabbi teach the prospective convert to read Hebrew, in actual practice only about 40 per cent of the Conservative rabbis fulfill this requirement.[2] After the period of study is concluded, the

Reform candidate for conversion is received into Judaism at a private religious service conducted by three rabbis. If three rabbis are not available, a rabbi and two congregational officers conduct the service. The Conservative rabbinate regards the Reform convert to be a valid convert. The Orthodox rabbinate does not.

Results

So much for the conversion process. What about the results? Again space does not permit more than brief answers to a number of key questions.

How many non-Jews are now being converted to Judaism annually in the United States? The average Conservative rabbi is converting one non-Jew a year. The average Reform rabbi is converting two non-Jews a year. Between 1500 and 1750 non-Jews are being converted each year by the Reform and Conservative rabbis of the United States. The number of non-Jews converted annually by American Orthodox rabbis is not known. Since American Orthodox rabbis outnumber the combined strength of the Reform and Conservative rabbinates, it would seem reasonable to assume that at least 2000 non-Jews are being converted to Judaism in the United States each year and the actual figure may very well be 2500 or more.

Is the number of converts to Judaism increasing or decreasing? A careful analysis of the statistics presented by the rabbis indicates that the number of conversions is increasing slowly but steadily year after year.

How many of the converts are male and how many of them are female? Down through the years, the Reform rabbis report a consistent proportion of one male convert to every four female converts. The Conservative rabbis report also, quite consistently through the years, a proportion of one male convert to every six female converts. Why does Reform Judaism attract a higher proportion of male converts than Conservative Judaism? Part of the answer certainly must be that Conservative Judaism requires that male converts be circumcised while Reform Judaism does not. In individual rabbis' experiences, there are wide variations from these general norms. One Reform rabbi in Los Angeles reported that he had converted 15 males and only 5 females. Among the Conservatives, a Boston rabbi reported that he had converted 6 males and only 4 females. On the other end of the scale, a Reform rabbi reported that he had converted 40 females without converting a single male. A Conservative Long Island rabbi stated that he had converted 14 females and no males.

What percentage of present conversions are motivated by an impending or existing marriage to a Jewish person? The Reform rabbis answered: 94 per cent or 16 out of every 17 conversions. The Conservative rabbis answered: 96 per cent or 24 out of every 25 conversions. The first obvious conclusion is that the number of persons converted to Judaism in the United States for reasons other than marriage is very small, probably between 100 and 150 a year. The second, based on the mathematics of the situation, is that Reform Judaism attracts more such converts than does Conservative Judaism at the rate of about three to one. A third possible conclusion is that, small as is the number of these non-marriage-motivated conversions, it is still surprisingly large, since, up to the time I made this study in 1953, neither Conservative nor Reform Judaism had made the slightest attempt to attract non-Jews into their ranks but, on the contrary, both groups had done much to convince most inquirers that such persons were not wanted.

It should be mentioned, too, that, in answering this question, a number of rabbis testified that, while the overwhelming majority of the non-Jews whom they had converted would never have become Jews had it not been for the involvement of marriage, many of these non-Jews discovered for themselves, either before or after marriage, that they were emotionally, intellectually and spiritually attuned to the teachings of Judaism and, as a result, they voluntarily and eagerly requested admittance into the religious household of Israel.

What percentage of the converts join a synagogue? The Reform rabbis estimated them at 66 per cent, the Conservative rabbis at 64.

What percentage of converts rear their children as Jews? The Reform rabbis' estimate was 85 per cent, the Conservative rabbis', 93. The small-city rabbis stated that their converts, almost without exception, belong to the local synagogue and rear their children as Jews. Many of the big-city rabbis stated that their answers to the last two questions were probably quite inaccurate because they had not seen many of their converts since converting them and had no knowledge of their subsequent spiritual development.

How many cases were reported by the rabbis of converts who abandoned the Jewish religion entirely in later years? Nine Reform and two Conservative rabbis reported a total of fifteen such cases. These fifteen persons were attending Christian religious services and/or sending their children to Christian religious schools. We do not know, of course, how many cases were not reported.

How do the rabbis evaluate the "Jewishness" of the converts who are members of their congregations? They were asked to compare the Jewish loyalties and interests of the converts with those of the Jewish-born in their congregations. Ten per cent of the Reform rabbis stated that the born Jews were better Jews than the converts; 56 per cent—that both groups rated about even; and 34—that the converts were better Jews than the born Jews. The Conservative rabbis replied as follows: 18 per cent stated that the born Jews were better Jews than the converts; 56— that both groups rated about the same; and 26—that the converts were better Jews than the born Jews. The weight of the rabbinic opinion is, therefore, that the converts, as a group, are more faithful adherents to Judaism than the born Jews. If this is so in a situation where approximately 95 per cent of the converts come to Judaism through marriage, one may assume that were most converts attracted to Judaism by a knowledge of its theology, philosophy and culture, without marriage being involved in any way, the contrast would be even greater.

To conclude: Are the converts whom we are now getting a spiritual asset or a spiritual liability? There can be no doubt about the composite opinion of the 785 Conservative and Reform rabbis who participated in the study from which I have quoted the statistical results: These converts are a precious spiritual asset. They challenge the Jewish-born to be more worthy of the priceless spiritual possession which has been given them by their fathers. They are a constant reminder of the Jew's neglected obligation to share this possession more unselfishly with those non-Jews who are dissatisfied with the faiths of their fathers and yearning for a more meaningful explanation of human existence and a more satisfying way of life.

There are growing indications in the Jewish world that long-held negative attitudes about converts and conversion are beginning to change. The day may not be far off when many Jews will begin to make it their spiritual business to let others know what we believe and to make them aware that if they come, voluntarily and sincerely and wholeheartedly, to join our religious community, they will be given a sincere and wholehearted welcome.

1. Other articles by the author dealing with this same subject-area include: "Conversions to Judaism by Reform and Conservative Rabbis", *Jewish Social Studies*, Vol. 16, No. 4, October 1954, pp. 299-318.

"A New Look at Conversion and Marriage", *Central Conference of American Rabbis Journal*, January 1957; also reprinted in *Jewish Digest*, March 1958.

"What Is a Jew?", *Central Conference of American Rabbis Yearbook*, Vol. 69, 1959, pp. 240-247.

2. This and all other statistical statements in this presentation are based on the findings of a research project I conducted a number of years ago among the Conservative and Reform rabbis of this country.

INTERMARRIAGE AND CONVERSION
ON THE AMERICAN COLLEGE CAMPUS

by
Richard L. Rubenstein

Few problems concern the Jewish community more directly than that of intermarriage. On it hinges the community's continuing ability to maintain itself. Religious conversion provided the Middle Ages with its principal mode of exit from Judaism. The rise of modern racial anti-Semitism has caused Jews seeking to leave Judaism to look for more viable means. Today Jewish identity is more often progressively diluted than officially and ceremonially terminated. Intermarriage has replaced religious conversion as the principal means of departure from Jewish life. However, the desire to leave Judaism is by no means the only reason for intermarriage. For some, intermarriage actually provides the instrumentality for a deliberately chosen entry into Judaism. For still others, it is the culmination of deep and lasting attachments formed by young people almost against their will. In such cases differences of background and faith recede before the greater power of human love. Of one thing we may be sure, intermarriage is

122

here to stay; the problem is not how to prevent it; it is how to cope with it.

There will always be a correlation between intermarriage and college life. People of varying faiths are thrown together in greater intimacy and with greater persistence at the college level than at most other periods of their lives. One need only contrast the relative social isolation of religious groups which characterizes adult American social life with the more open social possibilities of university life to realize this. In addition, college and graduate school students are at an age when permanent attachments are most likely to be formed. Increasingly, adult marriages have their origins on campus.

A great deal of useful information can be gathered from statistics concerning the relative incidence of intermarriage. That work is being carried forth ably by others. However, since intermarriage is a very concrete human problem involving the conflicting emotions of young people and parents, much can also be learned about it as it presents itself in counseling. Often case histories give insight not otherwise available. It is this aspect of the problem, rather than the admittedly important statistical or sociological work done by others, which is discussed here.

One such case history concerns a young lady who sought my guidance while I was at Harvard. She was a junior at Radcliffe, of upper class Protestant background. Her parents were extremely well to do and well connected. When she visited my office for the first time, she told me that she was interested in learning more about Judaism and asked that I recommend some good books for her reading. I had had enough experience to know that more than intellectual curiosity was involved. Several days later she returned and told me that she wanted to convert. She asked me how long the procedure would take and what it would involve. When I told her that it would take between three and six months at a minimum, she became very upset and insisted that such a period was altogether too long. I asked her why she could not wait. She answered: "I'm pregnant and we have to get married right away."

Obviously, I had little choice in the matter. Within a month the conversion lessons had been completed and the wedding celebrated. During the period of instruction, I saw the girl more frequently than I would have under normal circumstances. I learned that about two years before she had given birth to another child which had been the result of a union with another Jewish boy. That child had been given up for adoption. Normally, a clergyman doesn't ask questions such as "Why didn't you use protection?", but it was obviously appropriate in the situation. I was aware of the clinical hypothesis that many "accidental" pregnancies are not accidents at all but represent the unconscious desire of the participants to have a child. This may be due to a desire on the part of the girl to revenge herself against her parents for real or imagined hurts. It may bespeak unconscious rivalry with the mother. It may represent an unconsciously sought degradation. The motivations might vary, but from this perspective, some volitional element is involved in all such pregnancies.

When I asked the girl about her lack of precaution, she replied: "We thought nothing would happen just this one time."

"But it wasn't one time. This is the second time you thought nothing would happen. It's also the second time you thought nothing would happen with a Jewish boy," I replied.

Her answer seemed to bear out my suspicion that there were volitional elements involved in the pregnancy. On the face of it, one would imagine that a girl who had on another occasion given birth to a child out of wedlock would be doubly careful. Yet, she insisted that she was convinced nothing would happen. It was apparent to me that she not only wanted to be made pregnant but wanted it done by a Jew. She was, incidentally, a young lady of superior intelligence and background.

Shortly thereafter, I received a midnight telephone call from the mother of the boy. She was quite beside herself. As with most parents, her first demand was that I break up the relationship. I replied that the only basis on which I could continue to be of help was if the couple could trust me without any fear of my hurting their relationship. Should they feel that I had rejected them, they might easily turn to a Christian clergyman.

This sent the woman into a tirade against the girl. She claimed that the young woman was immoral and indecent for her past conduct as well as for getting her son into the present unpleasantness. I replied that this sort of activity required two willing participants and that the responsibility was mutual.

The mother said that her son had gone to Hebrew school, had had a fine Bar Mitzvah, and was a very good Jewish boy. She didn't see how this sort of thing could have happened to him. She had obviously been deeply wounded by the affair. She had tried to "do the best for her son," in her own lights. Somehow, she felt she was to blame and that the affair was basically degrading. Her reaction was consistent with that of most parents whom I have counselled. Perhaps the most important reason for their own bitterness and occasional intransigence was their unspoken feeling of guilt that, somehow, it was all their fault. What they did not understand was that, though they had undoubtedly failed as parents at some level, their failures were seldom different from those of parents of young people who did not intermarry. The feelings of guilt had a reality basis though seldom, if ever, for the particular situation which confronted us.

The distraught mother also failed or was unwilling to understand that a very human problem had to be met expeditiously and with a measure of *sang froid*. The young people had rejected both abortion and adoption as solutions. This in itself was a sign of health. Having acted with great irresponsibility, they were nevertheless ready to accept responsibility for the entailments of their so casually entered relationship. Yet, it was also plain that this marriage would need a great deal of help if it was to prove viable. Without it, the couple would very soon descend to hating and, at the very least, saying some very unkind things to each other. This would be accentuated by the fact that the young man had had definite plans of entering professional school. Without parental help, now needed more than ever, he would never achieve his professional ambition as a result of a casually commenced liaison. The sexual act occurred within a week of the couple's first acquaintance. One could also detect a very strong element of ambivalence towards Jews in the girl's makeup. True, she had twice been impregnated by Jews, but this was hardly proof against the development of a very strong anti-Semitism. Women frequently enter such relationships in order to degrade themselves and their families. Similar mechanisms are often at work in liaisons between white women and Negro men. As the need for self-degradation wore out, resentment against the husband as the imagined source of degradation could create a host of thoroughly unpleasant situations.

Above all, there was the unborn child, soon to become the innocent victim of desires, resentments and fantasies for which it was in no way responsible. I felt then as always that, since the child would have a Jewish father and a Jewish name, it was important that he receive a Jewish upbringing and be able realistically to face the many vicissitudes of Jewish existence which he would encounter. As a result, I consented to one of the shortest courses of study for conversion I have ever permitted. Before the actual marriage occurred, I saw both sets of parents separately and obtained their agreement to give the young people the necessary support for the completion of the young man's graduate studies. It was also decided that funds would be made available for the psychotherapy which the couple badly needed. Fortunately, both sets of parents were people of means and this presented no difficulty once the initial shock had subsided. When last heard of, the couple had learned much about themselves through psychotherapy and there was at least a fighting chance that the child would grow up in a healthy family.

This particular case illustrates a number of things about the problem of intermarriage and conversion. Above all, it is apparent how difficult it is to apply traditional norms to many such relationships. According to traditional practice, the desire to marry a Jew is one of the least praiseworthy motives for conversion. Furthermore, the attitude of the rabbi is to be what may be termed discouraging-encouragement. The rabbi must make plain the many disadvantages of fidelity to Jewish tradition and the severity of its disciplines, while offering the potential convert insight into Judaism's moral and spiritual values. Furthermore, he must diligently ascertain the real willingness of the convert to submit to the disciplines of Jewish tradition. In the instance under discussion, no attempt was made to dissuade, nor was personal religious practice a relevant issue. The conversion was executed with the greatest dispatch. The overriding fact was the forthcoming birth of the child and the conviction that it was in the child's best interest to be brought up as a Jew. By marrying a Jew, the convert had in effect become a part of the fate and destiny of the Jewish community. The conversion could not be described as conversion in the traditional religious sense, even though all of the traditional rituals of conversion, including ritual immersion, were observed. It could better be described as *adhesion* to the Jewish community rather than *conversion* to Jewish religion. Almost all of the twenty situations I have dealt with which led to conversion could be so described.

Adhesion could later result in conversion, especially where it entailed the forsaking of a strong Christian religious background. In such cases a religious vacuum had to be filled. In some instances, former Catholics became observant Jews far surpassing the expectations or even the real desires of their Jewish partners. This would indicate that the psychological disposition towards religious observance does not disappear with a change of religion. When, through conversion, old religious instrumentalities are forsaken, this type of personality does not change but appropriates those instrumentalities available in the new setting. This can frequently lead to much bitterness and misunderstanding. In many instances, conversion is undertaken only when it is learned that a Jewish marriage alone will appease the Jewish parents. Since there can be no Jewish marriage without conversion, conversions are sometimes begun as a means of solving *pro forma* the problem of Jewish marriage.

The couple often fails to apprehend that the conversion lessons constitute a dynamic situation whose outcome can never be determined at the outset. In many instances, the convert becomes far more aware than the Jewish partner of the complex factors involved in the decision to marry outside one's original faith. Often a heightened commitment to the real obligations of the relationship results. This may in part be due to the relationship with the rabbi. This in many ways resembles the psychoanalytic analyst-patient relationship, even where the rabbi's goals absolutely preclude analytic delving in depth. Furthermore, the conversion interview brings the convert into far more personal contact with the rabbi than the Jewish partner who is in some real sense a third party to the new situation. As a result, religious commitments and attitudes sometimes develop which have considerable intensity and which threaten the Jewish partner. Often there is a conflict between the expectations of the Jewish partner, who really wants a non-Jewish mate, and the increasingly Jewish attitudes and practices of the convert. Since Jewishness is in part a human response to a particular cultural situation rather than something inherited with one's genes, Jewish attitudes can be acquired in a surprisingly short time by those who come to participate in the Jewish situation.

It would also seem likely in the case under consideration that *the decision to acquire a Jewish mate was made prior to any contact with an actual Jewish partner.* This does not mean that a conscious and deliberate decision to marry a Jew had been made. Nevertheless, the behavioral patterns suggest that an unconscious decision had preceded the actual decision. It was almost as if the particular young man had very little to do with the matter. In almost all of the relationships it became apparent in counseling that the decision to marry a Jew was prior to the actual selection of the particular mate. During the course of the three months to a year in which I met with the converts, I came to learn a great deal about them. Although my goals precluded the use of psychoanalytic technique in counseling (free association was absolutely ruled out and all counseling took the form of face to face personal encounter), my own training was such that I could not be unmindful of the psychodynamic factors involved in the decisive personal commitments which were being made.

In this particular case, though the situation could not be reduced to traditional norms, something could be salvaged. There are others in which this cannot be said. One such situation which was called to my attention involved a Jewish college girl who had been made pregnant by an Irish Catholic boy. Abortion was considered and rejected. The alternatives were marriage or giving the child up for adoption. Both refused to convert or marry. The child was therefore given up for adoption. The violence implicit in this rejection of an utterly innocent child creates a human situation with few decencies. This situation is repeated several hundred times every year by Jewish girls in New York City who have children out of wedlock with Negroes. These are the only children of Jewish birth who cannot be placed for adoption in Jewish homes. In the majority of these situations, the symbolic uses of sex in fantasies of revenge, degradation, inversion of standards and parental rejection culminate only in the bitter and decisive rejection of those least to blame, the children.

Another case history which illustrates some of the continuing patterns of the problem involved a girl of upper-class Protestant background. Incidentally, most of the cases in which the non-Jewish partner became a convert involved Protestants. Where Catholics were involved, they were usually very insistent that, whatever the religious affirmations of the Jewish partner, the marriage be performed by a priest and the children brought up as Catholics. In almost every case of a Jewish-Catholic marriage, the children were lost to Judaism. In Jewish-Protestant marriages, I have always felt that I had a good chance of convincing the couple that it was best to enter the Jewish community as a family, unless the decision to marry a non-Jew was a step deliberately undertaken in order to leave Judaism. The young lady had been a member of the Junior League in her home city. At the age of ten, she had been sent to a midwestern psychiatric clinic by her parents who regarded her as disturbed. At the clinic she was under the care of a Jewish analyst whom she saw nearly every day for several years. She was a girl of high cultural attainment, very bright and very attractive. The Jewish boy she planned to marry seemed dull by comparison. His basic inclinations were to enter his father's business and to create a world of petty securities for himself. He wanted her to become Jewish mainly to placate his family and to have a Jewish wedding. I suspected almost from the start a basic incompatibility.

About midway in her studies, the young lady told me that she had broken off her engagement, but that she still wanted to become Jewish. At one level it was apparent that, though she was prepared to terminate her relationship with her fiancé, she was not prepared to terminate her relationship with the rabbi.

My reaction to her plea was an insistent refusal. She persisted. She claimed that on the basis of her studies she believed in Judaism and that she wanted to be Jewish. From the traditional point of view, it would seem that this would be the best kind of conversion, one unmotivated by any consideration of marriage or anything other than pure respect for Judaism. From my point of view, this was the worst reason for becoming Jewish. If all that was involved was an intellectual or religious assent to Jewish principles, it would seem that she ought rather to become a liberal Protestant. Conversion seemed less and less a religious decision and more and more *adhesion* to a religio-ethnic community.

I expressed myself to her rather emphatically: "Look, you can continue to see me and study Judaism as frequently as you like, but I refuse to authorize your conversion until you get yourself another Jewish boy."

This seemed very strange to her and she asked me to explain myself. "Well, the way you are now, you are obviously very Protestant and Anglo-Saxon in appearance. If you tell people that you are Jewish, both Jews and Gentiles alike are going to regard you as odd. Gentiles won't want you because you've turned Jewish; Jews will suspect you because they'll think you are strange. I am more interested in your finding a proper husband than in whether you ultimately become Jewish or Christian. If you really want to become Jewish, find yourself another Jewish boy, become engaged, and then I'll be delighted to authorize the conversion. However, I see certainly no necessity for you to marry someone outside of your own background."

She continued to see me weekly for about two months. Then one afternoon she brought a young Jewish professor into the office and introduced me to her new fiancé. Several months later she was converted and married. I always have been convinced that this young woman's unconscious decision to marry a Jew received its first impetus during her childhood treatment by her Jewish analyst. In her mind, she had two fathers, a good Jewish father who had lovingly accepted her, and a "bad" gentile father who had "rejected" her. It made very little difference that the real father's decision to send her to the clinic was undoubtedly a loving decision made with much heartache. From her childlike perspective, he had rejected her. During the course of the conversion interviews, I felt that I had an obligation to make her aware of this aspect of her decision. As I elicited an understanding of this from her, I came to realize that the child's original neurotic decision could no longer be cancelled by insight. It had become *functionally autonomous*. As a result of her therapy her total life-situation had become somewhat "Jewish." She experienced both the alienation and the inner insight which frequently accompanies being a partial stranger to what one knows best. She was no longer like the girls in her peer-group and could never again take seriously the things which concerned them.

Another contributing factor in her choice of a Jewish

husband and her ultimate rejection of her first Jewish fiancé seemed to have been her psychoanalysis. People who
have been in psychoanalysis often regard themselves as "in
the club." They feel, rightly or wrongly, that they have
achieved insights into dimensions of their personalities
which go far beyond those normally available. The psycho-
analyzed personality normally functions as a compliant
member of his community, living up to the role-expecta-
tions and affiliations to which he has committed himself.
Nevertheless, this compliance is dialectically related to a
very real alienation. In the analytic process, much of what
the analysand deeply believes is called radically into question. The very apt Hegelian expression for what transpires
is that the old alienations or negativities are "sublated"
(aufgehoben) in the newly achieved integration. This
means that in the new integration one does not entirely
identify with the roles and affiliations now accepted but
previously rejected. One accepts their necessity and their
inevitability. One makes the most of them, though something of the estrangement is never lost. One ends estrangement only by ceasing to be a stranger to oneself. One realizes the necessity of one's commitments. The transpar-
ency of social symbolism and myth no longer threatens to
destroy personality because one no longer depends entirely upon them. Alienation is overcome; one belongs and
does not belong at the same time, but one realizes that
there is absolutely no other viable choice. One returns to
one's first commitments, but with a difference.

It is not surprising that sensitive gentiles who have gone
through this experience should so frequently chose intellectually and artistically competent Jews as their marital
partners. At least half of the girls whom I have converted
have either been in psychoanalysis or psychoanalytic psychotherapy. In general, these girls were among the most
sensitive and the most competent young women I have

counselled. Somehow they saw their new situation as in some sense "Jewish". Of course, their Jewishness did not consist in a relish for the gastronomic folkways of Jewish culture. It consisted in the recognition of the Jewish intellectual as sharing their alienations, their insights, and their commitments.

In the past few years, a number of people prominent in the entertainment field have converted to Judaism, either as a matter of personal decision or as a result of marriage. While it is difficult to understand the inner motivations of people whom one has never met, there is one element present in all of the entertainers which is not unlike that of the young people I have met. No matter how well rewarded entertainers may be, no matter how close they are to people in high places, no matter how frequently their public and private lives are the subject of public comment and concern, entertainers remain outside the mainstream of society. The irony of their situation is that their talent brings them both recognition and estrangement. They have no fixed and established place in the social order. This is an advantage during periods of rapid upward social mobility. However, more than one entertainer has experienced the disappointment of discovering how insecure is the position in which he finds himself. Very frequently, Jews also find that their recognition and their status is conditional upon the market value of their talent. Intellectual talent is by no means as volatile a commodity as theatrical talent. Nevertheless, the pangs of belonging and rejection which afflict one group afflict the other. Under the circumstances, there is at least the possibility that those who intuit an inner connection between their own precarious and ambivalent situation and that of the Jews will, on occasion, seek to formalize this inner connection through conversion.

The desire to join the community of the alienated was brought home to me by one of my converts who came from a long line of New England ministers and teachers. She had belonged to all of the proper Protestant organizations in her town as she grew up. She had an accepted place in the best society of her community, and, yet, her place was of a very different order than that of the established families whose position was fixed by inheritance. As she matured and as her intellectual interests developed, she became more and more convinced that she did not belong. She knew that this was an element in her choice of a Jewish partner.

On one occasion, her comment on her interest in marrying a Jew elaborated on this theme. "I don't belong and the Jews don't belong, but at least they have each other," she said.

Sometimes the feeling that Jews have been acculturated in such a way that they are emotionally prepared for and capable of handling alienation arouses envy among non-Jewish intellectuals who are thrown into the company of Jewish colleagues. A number of them have on occasion complained to me that they did not really feel "in the swing" because they were not Jewish. One former Unitarian minister who had married a Jewish girl was emphatic in expressing this feeling. He said that something inside of him had always wanted to become Jewish but that he had at least settled for marrying a Jewish girl. In this instance, there was no conversion.

Alienation is by no means only a Jewish phenomenon. In truth, one can say that the human condition is essentially one of alienation. One does not have to be Jewish to experience it. Perhaps all that is necessary is a certain openness and sensitivity to the inevitable ironies of existence and an unwillingness to deceive oneself—an absence of what Sartre refers to as *mauvaise foi*. For those who do experience deeply, Jewish life may frequently seem attractive because it presupposes with great explicitness the fact of estrangement. The response of one convert made this apparent. As part of the course of my work, I asked her whether she was prepared to leave the relative security of the Protestant in-group and bring up her children with the relative insecurities of the Jewish out-group.

Her reaction to my query was that the Jews were by no means the only people who did not belong. At an important level this was true of any sensitive person. The difference was that in the Jewish situation it had been made explicit. For her part, she regarded the explicitness of the Jewish life as a distinct advantage.

The idea that estrangement could be one of the most important preconditions of interest in a Jewish marital partner and ultimately of conversion to Judaism casts its own light on the relative social isolation of the Jew. The academic community is undoubtedly one of the most open social communities in American life today. Yet, it is in large measure as closed and inwardedly divided as any other part of American life. Although there have been strong attempts to break down the walls of discrimination within fraternities, the kind of "integration" which has been achieved can largely be described as "token." Students and faculty alike meet cordially in classroom and administrative endeavors and then retire to their mutually exclusive Jewish and Gentile social worlds. For many students the existence of such mutually exclusive social worlds serves as a real deterrent against choosing a marital partner of another faith. My own experience has convinced me that the very existence of two distinct social communities frequently acts as a contributory factor making for intermarriage. The very existence of a wall poses its own invitation for some to scale it.

The most obvious way in which this works is the fact that that which is strange or different always seems more interesting and exciting than that which is altogether familiar.

Many of my counselee's have told me how they recoiled with horror at the thought of marrying "the boy next door." Some of them came from communities of very limited horizons. After involvement in the life of a major university, it is often very difficult for a young person to return to a small town with a relatively stable and homogeneous population. Very frequently, this estrangement from the home community is the first step which ultimately culminates in intermarriage.

Sexual factors are also at work. Often Jewish college boys are under the illusion that "Gentile girls are hotter." They use somewhat less refined expressions to convey the same meaning. Presumably, a candid conversation with Gentile college boys would reveal the same illusion concerning Jewish girls. Most of the Gentile girls reflected the believe that "Jewish men make better husbands." Presumably, the relatively fixed place of Jews at the middle of the economic spectrum contributes to this belief. I also have the suspicion which I have never been able to prove that Jewish circumcision is magically seen as somehow bringing the young man's ardor to manageable and predictable proportions. This is not the white heat of an intense lover's passion, but these girls usually were looking for predictable husbands rather than passionate lovers.

In an article entitled "The Most Prevalent Form of Degradation in Erotic Life," Freud has commented on one of the erotic dilemmas of western man relevant to intermarriage.[1] The mother as first and most prized love object is forbidden by the incest taboo. To the extent that a girl reminds a boy of his mother, the conflict between intense attraction and unconscious incest fear prevents the full development of a mature sexual life. This often leads young people to seek sexual partners in those who present less of a conflict, those who least resemble the parent of the opposite sex. Perhaps this underlies the segregationist's fear that mixing of the races in public places will lead to private mixing. Apart from the fact that private mixing has been going on for a very long time, the segregationist may unconsciously reflect the extreme sexual attraction of Negroes against which he defends himself so pathetically and often so cruelly. As an experiment, when Jewish boys came to me with very blonde non-Jewish girls, I would say, "Undoubtedly your mother has dark brown or black hair." Invariably, my guess turned out to be correct. What was more interesting, however, was the disturbed reaction of the boys. Undoubtedly, there are many men who can be fully men only with women who do not remind them of their mothers. It can thus be seen that the existence of separate subcommunities is not only no barrier against intermarriage but, very frequently, is itself a contributory cause to it. Furthermore, the facts by no means support the supposition that all such marriages lead the Jewish partners out of Judaism and into the more dominant group. On the contrary, for many members of the majority group the out-group has its own special values and appeal.

There are, however, some young Jews who simply want to get out of Judaism. They see it as possessing no special value which would not be preserved by the general culture without a continuing Jewish community. They feel that the barriers which exist between them and non-Jews are meaningless. This feeling probably exists more strongly in academic and intellectual circles than among business people. Often the intellectually inclined young Jew will regard his parents' world as middle class and lacking in sensitivity. Should his enthusiasm for his intellectual world be shared by a young woman of another faith, there is little that could hold him to Jewish life. Sometimes, though not too frequently, Jewish girls are deliberately excluded as possible marital partners by Jewish men. This attitude is usually rejected by most who marry out of their faith as a means of leaving Judaism. They are convinced that religious differences are insignificant. By deliberately excluding Jews as possible partners, they invert the problem of religious difference and give it as much emphasis as those who remain loyal. Nevertheless, the principal mode of exit from the Jewish community today remains intermarriage. There is little or no likelihood that this trend will diminish. On the contrary, there is every likelihood that the number of "part-Jewish" or "of partly Jewish descent" Americans will increase in the foreseeable future. Only an institution as utterly distasteful to all decent men as the Nuremberg laws could conceivably diminish the number of Jewish-Gentile marriages in America.

Another factor making for the acceleration of intermarriage is the place of Jews in the occupational spectrum. Jews are very heavily represented in the intellectual and creative professions. The proportion of Jews who attend universities is very much higher than that of Protestants or Catholics. Although there are only 47,000 Jews in Pittsburgh which has a total city population of 800,000 and a metropolitan population of 2,500,000, it seems as if half of those present at any concert of the Pittsburgh Symphony were Jews. This is also true of other cultural events. The proportion of Jews in the better graduate schools is extremely high. In some of the best known graduate schools it reaches as high as 50 per cent of the total enrollment. The higher the level of advanced studies and research, the greater the proportion of Jews in attendance. This means that a Gentile who reaches graduate school is far more likely to meet Jews sharing his vocational and intellectual interests than at the college or high school level.

In the case of women, graduate school is often a period of intense anguish. Dr. Carl Binger, writing on "The Pressures on Today's College Girl" in the March 1961 *Atlantic Monthly,* observed that the real objective of most women in graduate school is marriage. This objective is sharpened by the inevitable anxiety which every wedding announcement from former classmates brings. The female graduate student is under the additional handicap that it is extremely difficult for her to marry a man of lesser educational achievement or intellectual ability. This limits the field of available men to fellow graduate students or young faculty members. A lonely graduate student from a small town in her mid or late twenties is rarely going to be stopped from marrying an available and willing man because he is Jewish. While at Harvard, about a third of the women whom I counselled for conversion had already received their Ph.D.'s. As we know, doctors frequently marry nurses. Jews constitute about twenty per cent of the total enrollment of American medical schools; only an infinitesimally small percentage of the enrollment of American nursing training programs represents Jewish enrollment. The results are all too well known. The concentration of Jews in intellectual and professional fields thus very frequently throws them together with non-Jewish women for whom their availability and attainments more than compensate for their lack of in-group social status.

The problem of intermarriage is a permanent one in American-Jewish life. Undoubtedly, this is partly due to the fact that Americans participate in a free and open society. People who are free to choose their own friends are also free to marry them. Those who find the inevitability of intermarriage too distasteful even to contemplate forget that it is one of the prices one must pay for the freedom and the equality of American life. There can be no doubt that, given the choice, the vast majority of American Jews would prefer freedom and the risk of intermarriage to legal restrictions and enforced social isolation.

It is also clear that intermarriage does not necessarily destroy Judaism or the Jewish community. Judaism represents a very special value in American life. The creative use of alienation attracts many non-Jews to Judaism. With surprising frequency, it can result in conversion. Oddly enough, the loss of fixed dogma and explicit disciplines in modern Judaism has not created an end to conversion. It is often the person for whom all religious symbols have become transparent who converts to Judaism—; in reality, he or she adheres to the Jewish situation which he recognizes as the institutionalization of his own. He does not accept a new set of dogmas to replace others which can no longer be accepted.

If the real problem is seen as how to cope with intermarriage, there are realistic steps which can be taken by community leaders when faced with actual situations involving young people of different faiths. The first step remains that of making the young people aware of the inherent difficulties involved in such an undertaking. Should this fail, as indeed it usually will, the burden of intention should be that of winning the non-Jewish partner to conversion. In all instances, marriage is the best rather than the worst reason for conversion today. Young people create the first nucleus of community life by forming a family. They share each other's fate and destiny. It is best that this be shared within a common religio-ethnic community. Since most intermarriages are between Gentile women and Jewish men, it is best that the family's community be that of the husband. In our society a woman's social position is almost entirely dependent upon her husband. Under no circumstances should young people be encouraged to leave the question of religious affiliation open and subject to the later decision of the offspring. That places an unduly harsh problem of loyalties and identity on children and adolescents at an age when they can least tolerate such stresses.

While conversion lessons cannot change the convert's basic identity, they can give the convert insight into the kind of community he or she is to enter. Frequently, the lessons provide an opportunity for the convert to work out some of the inevitable tense moments which arise. Daughters-in-law do not have to be of another faith to have difficulties with mothers-in-law. It is important that an impartial and objective third party be on hand to effectuate the transition. In the long run, life has its own way of evoking sincere adhesion to the religio-ethnic group to which one joins oneself. Jewishness is not something racial. As we have suggested, psychological Jewishness can develop with surprising speed in the convert.

Our world is hardly one in which all of the given alternatives are black and white. Frequently, the realistic alternatives before people represent compromises. It is very easy to pontificate on the evils of intermarriage. It is somewhat more difficult to deal with the problem intelligently. Above all it must be remembered that in every birth there is not only new life, but also new hope. Whatever may be the difficulties in intermarriage, with proper training and insight many of the couples will form the nuclei of families whose children may become vital participants in the life of the Jewish community. Furthermore, the inevitable wounds which parents experience, no matter how they try to suppress these feelings, can at least be mollified when parents become grandparents. The problem is by no means one of total loss to the Jewish community.

1. Sigmund Freud, *Collected Papers*, transl. Joan Rivière, (London: The Hogarth Press and the Institute of Psycho-Analysis, 1925), Vol. IV, pp. 203-216.

INTERMARRIAGE IN THE SMALL COMMUNITY

by Ralph M. Weisberger

THE PROBLEM: Serious but not hopeless. The convocation of this conference on "Intermarriage and Jewish Life," is a recognition of the gravity of the problem. The situation is serious, and the possibility of an increasing trend of out-marriages away from the Jewish fold is a disquieting one. Is the future existence of the Jewish people in jeopardy? If the leaders of the "large" Jewish communities are worried, how much more precarious would seem to be the state of the "small" community.[1] Are these communities doomed to extinction? Their problem is great and their status uncertain, yet the picture is not completely gloomy or hopeless. As there are factors which drive people to intermarriage, so there are factors which may help to control and perhaps even to reduce it.

CHANGE IN ENVIRONMENT: From Ghetto, to Assimilation, to Isolation. The modern Jew is brought into much closer contact with non-Jews than ever before. On the street-level of this building in which the Conference meets is a restaurant whose menu illustrates this change. In the window a placard boasts that each evening a different

143

"Continental" dinner is offered. Monday is Irish night, Tuesday belongs to the Hungarians, Wednesday is Israeli night; Thursday caters to Germans, Friday to Americans, Saturday to Italians, and Sunday honors the French. Each evening's menu is identified by the flag of that nation. This epitomizes the multi-ethnic, even cosmopolitan, environment in which we live today. A Jew need not seek it out; it is thrust upon us.

In eastern Europe, most Jews lived on a "mainland", a concentration of fellow-Jews. Many villages and small towns were predominantly Jewish. Only the disrespected *"yishuvnik"* deigned to live far out in the country, away from the community, and he was ridiculed for his ignorance and simplicity. A few Jews worked for, or were in contact with, Gentiles, but they lived among those of their faith. Only the occasional *"shtadlan"* (spokesman for a Jewish community) came into immediate and personal relationship with the ruling powers of a locality. Even he might bring along to the nobleman's court enough fellow-Jews to provide a *"minyan"* (quorum) for religious services, and a *"shohet"* for ritual slaughtering. He provided a "ready-made" community or congregation, to assure his Jewish identity. In America, the environment changed to one in which assimilation was made much easier. Large cities, even Suburbia, may have neighborhoods which are predominantly or significantly Jewish. Assimilation with non-Jewish neighbors or in business circles occurs, but there is a scattering of "large islands" of Jewish identity. In the small community, however, this scattering amounts to an almost complete isolation from Jewish identification. The individual here is like a man in a lone lifeboat on the open sea who endeavors to chart his course so that he will remain in touch with the "mainland" of Jewish life and not be lost in the deep waters of intermarriage. He meets non-Jews not only in business and in school, but on every level and in every phase of daily activities—in the social, cultural and political arenas. There is a gathering or a committee meeting in the Garden Club, Rotary or Kiwanis Club, Literary Society, Chamber of Commerce, or Community Chest; the Jew may even be a leader in these circles, yet he is isolated.

SIZE OF A "SMALL COMMUNITY": The largest Jewish community in the world is found in New York City, where over two million Jews make up nearly 30 per cent of the population. Compared to this, Philadelphia's one-quarter million Jews, who make up 10 per cent of the population, may be considered small. In the sense of this report, however, "small" means a handful of families in the community. A former resident of such a community in South Carolina addressed a group of the Conservative Women's League on her experience as a schoolgirl there. As reported in the *Jewish Digest* magazine, she told them of her place in her high school class. Among 307 graduates, she was the lone Jewish girl. This is what "small" means.

LOCATION OF COMMUNITIES: While serving as military chaplain during World War II, I visited communities in Florida, North Carolina, Tennessee and Mississippi. More recently, my work as circuit-riding rabbi for the North Carolina Association of Jewish Men took me through North and South Carolina and a part of Virginia. The size of the individual communities ranged from a few families to about twenty. When organized into congregations to be served by the circuit-rabbi, the groups ranged from 15 to 30 families. A congregation of 30 families gathered its flock from eight different communities, from a few miles to 50 miles away from its synagogue. Thus, bringing a child from the most distant community to the religious school meant a journey to and fro of 100 miles. Another congregation took in Jews from five communities, altogether 23 families. But I am referring also to a somewhat larger com-

munity, that of Roanoke, Virginia, which consists of 250 Jewish families. The total population of the city, however, is 110,000, and the percentage of Jews is less than 1 per cent. This, too, must be considered a "small" community.
THE PEOPLE: Some of these small-town dwellers were born and raised in the South; some are displaced Northerners. Sometimes, servicemen who had military training in camps located in that section of the country met and married local girls. After the conclusion of the war, they settled down in a southern community. Other Northerners were brought down South by business interests, either temporarily as agents for Northern industries, or permanently on their own.
THE BIBLE BELT: This term denotes not only a greater interest in worship or Bible study, but also an unrestrained inclusion of sectarian, that is, Christian hymns and New Testament readings in the curriculum of the public schools. A housekeeper or servant working in a Jewish home may sing such hymns to the Jewish child and tell the boy or girl Christian stories. In school, the child learns to sing "Jesus Loves Me." In speaking to kindergarten children about Jerusalem and Israel during a Hebrew class, I asked: "What is the holiest country in the world?" The answer was, "Jesus." "What is the holiest city in the world?" Again the response was, "Jesus." In other words, to these Jewish children, 'holy" was synonymous with "Jesus". Does this Christian propaganda pressure lower the resistance of the Jew to marrying out of his faith? More than an isolated few think that it is perfectly acceptable for a Jewish child to recite "The Lord's Prayer." When told that this prayer was the heart of the Christian faith, the defense was, "Word for word, what's wrong with it, especially as you say that its ideas are based upon Jewish prayers?" Imagine the predicament of a child who was transferred from a school in a northern, "large" Jewish community to a southern,

"small" one in the Bible Belt. Her public school teacher related the story of the Crucifixion. "When he came to the Crucifixion and the Jews," she said, "I looked around the classroom, and all the children had a bad look on their faces. So, I put a bad look on my face, too." An insecure individual may tend to seek the favor of his non-Jewish neighbors, but possibly not to the extent of marrying out of faith. The young man who thought there was nothing wrong with reciting "The Lord's Prayer" travelled a few hundred miles to meet a Jewish girl. Often, the heavy hand of sectarian pressure may have the effect of pushing him back within his own fold and strengthen his self-respect as a Jew.

INTEGRATION: The problem of integration denotes either a negative or a positive influence. The Jew knows that the aversion of white Christians against the Negro may easily be turned against him and consequently he fears to speak out with the voice of the ancient prophets of Israel. The insecure man may even seek the favor of his prejudiced Christian neighbor. More probably, however, his self-respect will prompt him to realize that the best defense against any ill-will is to maintain his Jewish identity.

RELIGIOUS OUTLOOK: Is there a difference in intermarriage between Orthodox, Conservative and Reform Jews? A comment by Charles Angoff on this problem appeared in *The Jewish Spectator* of September 1959.[2] Upon visiting a Reform Congregation, he was surprised to find only fifteen members. He inquired of the rabbi whether it were due to intermarriage. The rabbi admitted that the situation was bad, but added that it had been worse. The extent of out-marriage was about 25 per cent among Jewish boys and girls, but ten years ago it had been 40 per cent. Among the Conservative and Orthodox in that community, it was considerable, too, but less. At one time out-marriage came to 15 per cent, but now was 10 per cent. This, of course, is a one-shot observation. In other localities, out-marriage may be greater among the children of orthodox families.

THE ROANOKE, VIRGINIA, COMMUNITY: This study was made by the rabbi of the only congregation in town, the conservative one, as a basis for his doctoral thesis.[3] As mentioned above, Roanoke has a population of 110,000 and a Jewish community of 250 families. Figuring the number of Jewish individuals to be about 1,000, we find that those of the Jewish faith comprise less than 1 per cent of the city. Of these 250 families, there were 45 mixed marriages, or 18 per cent of the total. The out-marriages were chiefly of Jewish men with non-Jewish women. In these cases, did we lose the man or gain the woman? Of the 45 mixed families, over one-half, namely 25, belonged to some Jewish organization. In these "small" communities, it is not uncommon to find a woman proselyte to Judaism through marriage who is active not only on the local scene, but also leading in state-wide activities of Jewish organizations. While serving as a military chaplain in Mississippi, I met such a proselyte who was the president of the Temple Sisterhood. She spoke with pride of raising funds to repaint the building. She requested some pamphlets on Judaism for her study group, with the explanation: "We like to study; we're not like them, who don't care to study." Whom did she mean by "we"? She meant the Jewish people whom she had adopted. Whom did she mean by "them"? These were the Gentiles, among whom she was born. This modern Ruth no longer considered herself part of the world of the Gentiles, but a stranger to their way of life. Similarly, of the 45 intermarried couples in Roanoke, more than half sent their children to Hebrew School and many expressed the desire that their children might marry Jews.

DIFFERING ATTITUDE OF THE SEXES: It is significant that of the 45 Jews in Roanoke who out-married,

41 were men, and only four were women. I believe that this is in accordance with a general tendency. One reason may be found in the high respect in which Jewish family life has been held throughout the ages. The Jewish girl doesn't want to give this up, but the Gentile woman, especially if she comes from the lower classes, is willing and, at times, anxious to be accepted into the supposedly privileged status which is enjoyed by a Jewish wife. Perhaps, too, parents exert more control over a child's choice of a mate in the case of a daughter than in the case of a son. Since the man is considered to be the aggressor, he may feel that it is his prerogative to request the non-Jewish woman to accept his Jewish faith. The woman, however, feels she must follow her husband, even to the point of putting up with his different religion, if not actually accepting it herself. The predominance of male over female out-marriages may seem surprising, considering the viewpoint of Jewish Law. According to *Halakha,* a child's religion in a mixed marriage is determined by the religion of the mother. The child of a Jewish mother is considered a Jew. Consequently, when a Jewish man marries a Gentile woman who does not accept Judaism, the children of that union are lost to Judaism, but when a Jewish woman out-marries and the Gentile husband does not accept Judaism, the children remain in the Jewish fold or can, at any rate, easily be returned to it. However, Jewish girls out-marry less than Jewish men. This whole area is largely unexplored and we offer here only stray observations.

POSITIVE FACTORS WHICH AID IN MAINTAINING JEWISH IDENTITY: In recent years, there has been a change in attitude of the Jewish male toward the different religion of a desired mate. Once, he might have felt himself to be the "inferior" party, who was being paid a favor, if he was "accepted" by a girl of the "superior" cultural group. Certain factors, however, which are too complex to be elaborated here, are now helping to bolster his cultural morale to the point where he not only is not surprised at his wife's acceptance of Judaism, but even requests this as a prerequisite to marriage. Apparently, he feels more secure now and as an equal.

IMPROVEMENT IN SECURITY—PHYSICAL, ECO-NOMIC, SOCIAL: Modern Jewish youth are economically more firmly established than their fathers once were. Socially, they are more "accepted" by their Gentile neighbors. While in past years the school fraternities considered a Jewish youth an outcast, today he may be invited to join. Jews may not only be members of community organizations, but even their leaders. Young Jews, born in America, no longer feel contact with Gentile youngsters to be a threat to their physical safety as their immigrant fathers might have. There is more self-assertion and self-assurance.

MILITARY SERVICE: In the armed forces, all religious faiths are officially recognized and enjoy equal status and rights. A Jewish chaplain carries the same authority as a Catholic or Protestant chaplain, although the Jews represent only 3 per cent of the men in uniform. There is no "minority" and "majority" relationship. Jewish religious services and holyday celebrations are publicized and held openly and the commanding officers attend them. The Jewish chaplain always carries his Star of David above the Ten Commandments (the chaplain's military insignia) openly. When the Jewish serviceman sees that, he feels that he is the equal of all other servicemen. He meets Gentile boys and lives in close quarters with them. He meets some Gentile girls in uniform, and others socially, either in camps or in the surrounding communities where he visits. These men attend Jewish services, not always because they are "religious", but because it strengthens their Jewish affiliation and gives them status and security in the eyes of their fellow-servicemen. These attitudes are carried over into civilian life, but it is difficult to say whether they increase or decrease the readiness to intermarry.

THE STATE OF ISRAEL: Pride in the new independence of the State of Israel, which now sits in the UN councils, has added to the self-respect and security of Jewish youth. The rabbi of Roanoke, Virginia, commented that a positive attitude towards maintaining Jewish affiliation was observable today, more so than ten or twelve years ago. As he made this remark, I did a bit of arithmetic. What had happened twelve years ago? The War of Liberation and the emergence of the State of Israel, of course. All minorities have taken courage from this event. While overseas in the Persian Gulf Command, I discovered that our Negro chaplain was deeply interested in Israel. He felt that if the Jewish people could do it, why not his own minority group? The Jew in the "small" community feels likewise. Israel is a tiny nation and a minority in the wide world. Courageously, nonetheless, it carries the Jewish name successfully. This is reflected by the individual Jew in a small community. Israel's pride is his pride and Israel's determination to survive is translated into a similar attitude in his own life. I have observed this on many occasions.

COMMUNITY ORGANIZATION: Small communities in North and South Carolina, which could not possibly maintain a permanent rabbi on their own, have been organized under the auspices of the North Carolina Association of Jewish Men. I carried on this work while visiting them periodically on a circuit basis. From five to eight tiny communities, containing a handful of Jewish families each, have joined hands to organize congregations of from 15 to 30 families and have built and maintained a synagogue. A reform synagogue which had been closed for 50 years was reopened to active use. Thus is their determination to survive. They keep asking, "Why do the larger communities forget us?" They want to remain a part of the community of Israel.

TZEDAKAH:[4] Contributions to a wide range of charitable causes mark the determination of the Jews in small communities to keep the "Jewish spirit" alive. Christian churches and general community projects are liberally supported. But Jewish institutions are never forgotten. Of course, Israel is dear to them and receives a generous response. They are flooded by *"meshulahim"* (religious charity collectors) and, in their desire not to overlook any worthwhile project, they give to all and thereby are occasionally victimized. One such collector entered a local store and requested a donation of $150. The clerk returned from the office with a check for only $50. The collector insisted on the larger sum, but in vain. Thereupon, he took his *tallith* (prayer shawl) out from his travelling bag and proceeded to parade around the store, thus embarrassing the owner. He was given the full amount he had requested.

RELIGIOUS OBSERVANCE: Some men conscientiously put on *tefillin* (phylacteries) every morning for prayer, to maintain the Jewish spirit in their homes. Some go to great effort and inconvenience to maintain a kosher home. In a larger community, one may simply be faced with the choice of buying or not buying kosher meats. In a small community, however, one may be located hundreds of miles from a kosher butcher or slaughterer. These difficulties are overcome by those interested in overcoming them. The *shohet* visits the community periodically, or the butcher ships meat, frozen or packed in dry ice. For a shorter trip, the meat is put on the bus at one end by the butcher and taken off at the other end by the recipient. The youth, who witness this interest in Jewish identity, surely must be influenced when they choose a mate. Only thus can they assure the survival of their family within the Jewish fold and prevent the extinction of the Jewish community in their town. The family in the small community resists an out-marriage not simply on religious or personal grounds but on those of Jewish survival. In a large community, one may "feel Jewish" vicariously, because of the size of the Jewish community. Where there are only a handful, if any, fellow-Jews, there is no vicarious identity. One must belong entirely or depart entirely.

INTER-DATING: This is not an academic problem, to be considered in the abstract, but a reality, to be faced, in the small community. Above we reported about the girl who was the only Jew in a high school graduating class of 307. What attitude must a Jewish parent practice in such a situation? Surely he must be a Solomon and a diplomat, a loving parent and a loyal Jew, yet not oppose inter-faith relationships. To be overly strict and to forbid inter-dating may mean social oblivion for the youth and lead to resentment and even rebellion. To withhold discipline and to permit indiscriminate dating may be an open invitation to out-marriage. The rabbis of old forbade socializing with the heathens in their day on the grounds that "drinking their wine will lead to sharing their bread, which will lead to marrying their daughters." Surely, this is a delicate tightrope to walk. The common understanding is: "Dating, yes; marriage, no." The problem of inter-dating is more aggravated than it used to be in former years, as there is less of a tendency to travel any considerable distance to meet a date now than there was in former years. At one time, it was not unusual for young men to travel 150 miles to get to a dance or meet dates. Now, there is more neighborly mingling of Jews and Gentiles, but also there are more region-wide gatherings of Jewish youth in groups. The young people are not overwhelmed by their problem. The Youth Advisor of the North Carolina Association of

Jewish Youth informed me that, when the youngsters assemble from all parts of North and South Carolina and Virginia and discuss their problems, that of intermarriage is not considered to be a serious one. They claim to understand their role in the ongoing drama of the survival of the Jewish people. For these youths, the choice of a college becomes an especially important decision. Aside from the usual factors, there is the additional question faced by parents in the small community: "Where will my child have a better chance of meeting and marrying a Jewish young man or woman?" With all ingenuity, the problem persists. *FINDING A JEWISH MATE:* The proverbial expression speaks of "finding a needle in a haystack." I think of this problem in terms of the navigator of an airplane finding the tiny islands of the Azores. They are situated in the Atlantic Ocean, midway between South America and Africa, and when I flew overseas during World War II, our plane landed there for refueling. When I saw the Azores on a world map, I wondered how it was possible for our navigator to have found such a tiny spot of land in the huge ocean. The same amazement was felt at learning how fate brought people together. While serving in Persia, a naval officer from the armed guard aboard a merchant ship told me the story of how he had met a Jewish family in Australia. It was a Friday and he felt homesick, so he took a walk aimlessly about the port. Soon his sense of smell was directing his steps. A familiar odor drew him on. Finally, he stopped where he smelled it strongest, knocked on the door and asked, "Would you by any chance be cooking *'gefilte fish'*, and are you Jewish?" The response was in the affirmative, to both queries. In Roanoke Rapids, North Carolina, I heard the story of how a girl from Boston enrolled in the university in Miami, Florida. She met a Gentile young man who wanted to marry her and she became engaged to him. However, during the summer, she visited with a Jewish family from Roanoke Rapids, Virginia, in their cottage at Virginia Beach, Virginia. There this family introduced her to a Jewish young man, whom she preferred and subsequently married. Her route led from Boston, Massachusetts, via Miami, Florida, to Virginia Beach, Virginia—and a Jewish marriage. In another community near Charlotte, North Carolina, I met a young man who had left New York City to become a partner in a business in this small town and had married a Gentile girl whom he divorced after two children had been born. This man took a business trip to Denmark. While sitting in a restaurant, a Danish girl was helpful to him and provided him with a desired information. It turned out that she was Jewish and he brought her back to America and to his tiny town of but a few thousand people and a handful of Jews. His route took him from New York to North Carolina to Denmark and back to North Carolina—now with a Jewish wife. It may well be that these cases are more frequent than we think.

CONCLUSION: There is a lot of syncretism in America and even confusion all around. Intermarriage can lead to complications, even with a humorous angle. In a small town, a Jew had married a Gentile girl who had not accepted Judaism, but who did accompany him to Jewish religious services. When her mother (his mother-in-law) became ill, I was asked to visit her, and I did. In the course of our conversation in the daughter's home, it turned out that just a few days ago she had been visited by another clergyman—her own Protestant minister. Frequently, one religion is considered as good as another.

The question of status looms large. It is said of Heinrich Heine that he despaired of his attempt to find peace in the Gentile world by giving up Judaism, and later by trying to readopt some kind of Judaism. Finally, somewhat plaintively, he resigned himself: *"Keine Messe wird man*

singen; keinen Kaddish wird man sagen." (In Louis
Untermeyer's translation: "There will be no whispered
Masses, none will rise to say the Kaddish.")[5] Christians
considered him a Jew and Jews considered him a Christian
while he considered himself a cosmopolitan.[6] In the small
community, the mature Jew realizes that his status and
self-respect are found among his own faith and people.

We must not minimize dangers, but we must not forget
that Jews are a stubborn people. Available statistics warn
us of the serious problem of losing 15 or 20 per cent of our
youth through intermarriage. As for the small community,
I think of the saying I heard from my mother, of blessed
memory, who quoted her grandmother: "The unusual
thing is not that people die, but the miracle is that they
live." So, I must admire the 80 or 85 per cent of small-
town Jews who hang on stubbornly, though I regret to
consider those we lose and wonder whether the tide can
be turned. Concerning those who do intermarry, I think of
the Yiddish story of the young man who married a Gentile
girl who accepted Judaism and then insisted that he, too,
begin to take his religion seriously and practice the cere-
monial observances. Finally, he complained to his mother
about it. Her reply was: "Who told you to marry a Gentile
girl and have her become a Jew? Why didn't you marry
a Jewish girl in the first place, so you wouldn't have all
this trouble?" Where there must be intermarriage, let us
hope we do not lose a son, but gain a daughter.

1. There is no extensive recent literature on Jews in small towns and
none at all that is focused on intermarriage. W. Lloyd Warner and Leo
Stole, *The Social Systems of American Ethnic Groups* (New Haven,
1945) is merely of peripheral interest in this context because "Yankee
City's" small-town Jewish community is not isolated from other Jewish
communities; neither is the Jewish community of Derby, Connecticut,
which is analyzed in Milton L. Barron, *People Who Intermarry* (Syra-
cuse, 1946). Lee J. Levinger, "The Disappearing Small-Town Jew",

Commentary (Aug., 1952), ranges far and wide in an impressionistic manner; Robert Shostek, *Small Town Jewry Tell Their Story* (Washington, D.C., B'nai B'rith Vocational Service Bureau, 1953) is not available in printed form. More pertinent are: Benjamin Kaplan, *The Eternal Stranger—A Study of Jewish Life in the Small Community* (New York, 1957); Peter Isaac Rose, *Strangers in Their Midst—A Sociological Study of the Small-Town Jew and his Neighbors* (Ph.D. Thesis, Cornell University, 1959), now available in *The Jewish Journal of Sociology*, Vol. III, Dec. 1961, 174-191; and Clare Wishner, "The Story of Gowanda," *The Chicago Jewish Forum*, Vol. 18, No. 1 (Fall 1959.) The locale of the Kaplan study is Louisiana; the two others were done in upstate New York. Although not systematically comparable and only tangentially dealing with intermarriage, these studies indicate a greater incidence of intermarriage in the earlier stages of Jewish settlement than in recent years, owing to the greater institutionalization of Jewish life which marks the last three decades; a greater resistance to intermarriage on the part of small-town Gentiles than on the part of small-town Jews; and a tendency among younger Jews in small communities to move to larger cities, thus exposing the remainder to increased isolation and renewal of the earlier trend toward intermarriage. Each one of these tendencies would deserve a separate investigation. (Editor's Note.)

2. Charles Angoff, "In the Margin", *The Jewish Spectator*, Vol. 24 (Sept. 1959), 21-24.

3. Tobias Rothenberg, *A Sociological and Educational Study of the Jewish Community of Roanoke, Va.*, (Diss., Jewish Theological Seminary of America, 1960).

4. The Hebrew word *"tzedakah"* stands for "charity," but in literal translation means "justice."

5. The Jewish prayer for the dead.

6. Actually, Heine is consoled by the thought that Mathilde, his "suesses, dickes Kind", will visit his grave at the Père Lachaise cemetery in Paris. (Editor's Note.)

PROBLEMS CONFRONTING THE RESEARCHER ON INTERMARRIAGE IN A METROPOLITAN AREA

by Jacob T. Zukerman and Alvin Chenkin

Although those of us who live in a large metropolitan area like Greater New York have heard of many cases of inter-marriage between Jews and non-Jews, we find ourselves in the dual position of possessing little exact knowledge of the extent of such intermarrying while being forced to resort to untested generalities about the causes of those that occur.

The only national estimate available to the researcher in this field is based upon the United States Census study of religious preferences reported by the civilian population of the United States in March of 1957. This study reported that 7.2 per cent of all married couples in which at least one spouse was Jewish was the result of inter-marriage.[1] However, from the viewpoint of investigating the proportion of married Jews married to non-Jews, the more meaningful percentage (after converting the census "couples" into number of individuals) might be in the neighborhood of 3.7.

This national estimate, based upon a relatively small sample, serves merely to set a floor under any estimate of the rate of Jewish out-marriage since it reflects only one aspect of intermarriage, viz., those couples whose religious differences are maintained after marriage. The Census study did not obtain figures for those couples where one spouse converted to the religious preference of the other. The 3.7 per cent rate would be higher by some unknown amount if we knew the number of couples now listed as Jewish where one spouse had converted *to* Judaism, and those couples now listed as non-Jewish where one spouse had converted *from* Judaism.

The few Jewish community studies which have incorporated questions on intermarriage indicate that the figure of 3.7 per cent derived from the Census study tends towards the low side even on the basis discussed above. In the Washington, D.C. study (1956) the intermarriage rate was given as 6.5 per cent; in New Orleans (1953) the rate was 7 per cent; in Jacksonville, Florida (1945) 6.5 per cent; although in Canton, Ohio (1955) the rate was given as under one per cent.[2] Differences in study methods and the degree to which the study process was designed to elicit this information make it difficult to evaluate the individual community variations. It is interesting to note in this connection that the files of the Family Location Service in New York (which specializes in family desertion cases) covering the last 4,000 families served in the past six years indicate that 4.7 per cent of the Jews involved had married non-Jewish spouses.

This then, is the first problem that the researcher must cope with in evaluating those factors in a metropolitan area, such as New York, which lead to intermarriage. While estimates of intermarriage among Jews are scarce, they are limited still further by the fact that they cover smaller Jewish communities or specialized socio-economic groupings.

The importance of Greater New York to this problem is due to the fact that the Jewish population of this area constitutes almost 50 per cent of the total Jewish population of the United States, and, at the same time, approximates more than 25 per cent of the general white population in the Greater New York area.[3] The Jewish population in this area is the most nearly "normative" group in the country in terms of income distribution, education, and occupation. Hitherto much of the research done on attitudes towards intermarriage has been attempted among students at colleges or other specialized groups. Such inquiries must, of necessity, scant the reactions of those Jews in the lower income and education groups represented most heavily in such Metropolitan areas as New York.

Some General Considerations

The very size of a community is of moment in our consideration, for in a city like New York with its 2-1/2 million or more Jewish residents, there is so much more opportunity for the Jewish youngster to meet a mate of the same religion, that the frequency of intermarriage is likely to be lower in the absence of other factors. Compare that with the town with only a dozen Jewish families and the lack of opportunity of the Jewish girl to find a Jewish lad to her liking. Yet we find that intermarriage does take place even in predominantly Jewish sections of Brooklyn and the Bronx. Can it be that there are other considerations which may be of effect? Is it possible that the larger the city, the more opportunity there is for anonymity and for independence of choice and therefore more opportunity for intermarriage? Shall we not investigate whether the Jewish community in a large metropolis is not composed of various sub-cultures rather than one homogeneous culture? Do members of some sub-cultures feel that they are incompatible with members of other sub-cultures? Do some sub-cultures make the act of intermarriage more the norm than the exception? There may be more questions of that kind.

We might also consider whether a large community like New York opens a wider avenue for deviance from accepted norms of behavior and for exercising forms of rebellion or emancipation which are not as available in a smaller city or in a more intensely concentrated Jewish environment. Does the protesting youth find in New York a place in which he can get away from his family and friends, yet remain a New Yorker and retain his job and professional connections and many of his cultural ties, even as he divorces himself from his "mishpocheh" by marrying out of his faith? Or is it more true, as some may suggest, that New York offers the rebelling or freedom seeking youth other forms of ventilation which diminish his need for expressing his revolt by intermarriage?[4]

In the San Francisco study of Jewish population (1959)[4] the proportion of marriages in which one spouse was a non-Jew was reported separately for three sections of the San Francisco area: the city of San Francisco proper, the Peninsula area and Marin County. The respective rates were approximately 9.4, 11.1, and 22.7 per cent. While the latter figure is much higher than the rate for the other two sections, it refers to 2,700 individuals out of the total of 66,000 covered in the study. However, other data from this study showed gross differences between Marin and the other two sections. For example, on religious identification, 43 per cent of Marin's population report "non-identifying" compared with 21.6 per cent (San Francisco) and 27.0 (Peninsula). It is clear that there are significant differences associated with various demographic variables. But this study leaves open the question as to whether the higher proportion of intermarriages in Marin occurred among those growing up in that area or whether those who intermarried moved there later because of greater acceptance.

On the other hand, we might wish to know a good deal more about the effect upon intermarriage of the movement towards the suburbs. If it is true, as we are told, that the Jews in suburbia tend to live as a more Jewishly conscious or even more ghettoized Jewish group, is there evidence, as yet, to show how this has affected the rate of intermarriage? Do Jewish youngsters in suburbia interdate more or less frequently? Does their attendance at more integrated high schools lead to more romancing with non-Jews? Or does their parents' apparent need for Jewish identification (so often this need has been nurtured by the parents' desire to have their children associate with other Jewish youngsters) carry over to the children in whose cause the parents have turned to Jewish communal living?

Specific Factors

Some of the more specific factors which we would like to see examined in terms of their quantitative as well as qualitative impact upon intermarriage are:

1. Does relative size of the Jewish Community within the metropolitan area have some bearing? Or is it the total number of Jewish families within the city that is more important? Are Jews located heavily in certain areas only and what effect does this have?

2. Is there a difference as to where the city is located?[5] Is it in the Northeast (with its 8.5 per cent of Jewish population and 69.1 per cent of all American Jews) or in the South (with its 0.8 per cent of Jewish population and 7.7 per cent of all American Jews) that there is more, or less, intermarriage?

3. Does the type of metropolitan area make a difference? What about its industries and businesses? Its cultural attributes?

4. Does it matter where the Jews live within the city?[6] Are there Jewish districts—how large are they, how old, how

fashionable? Is the Jewish area considered a "Ghetto", a vestige of the old days? Or do many Jews live in fully integrated, mixed areas, where religious and ethnic differences play less of a role? Do they live in an apartment or tenement house and with what kind of tenants? Is living in a large housing development more impersonal? Or is it a little village within a large city?

5. What is the degree of acceptance of the Jew in the community? How secure is the Jew of his acceptance in the area? Where on the socio-economic and cultural ladder does the Jewish family stand?

6. How did the youngster's education and early association relate to his eventual intermarriage? What kind of school did he attend, public, private, a Yeshivah, a Jewish day school? Who were his classmates and with whom did he play and associate—in his park, playground, or community center? Was he a member of an intersectarian club or group? Was his scout group based in a synagogue, church, or public school?

7. Is there a relationship to the degree of the individual's involvement in Jewish communal activities and interests in the Metropolitan community? Does this differ in larger cities from its effect in smaller towns? If the youngster was not educated in a Yeshiva or Jewish day school, did he receive supplementary Jewish education? Has he a knowledge of and/or interest in Jewish cultural activities —books, music, theatre, lectures, classes? Has he been active in a YMHA or Jewish Center or some Jewish fraternal organization or synagogue sponsored or based group? Is he interested in Zionism, in cultural-secularist Jewishness, in religious Jewish life? If so, how much of his time and devotion has been given to these activities; are they in addition to, or in place of, activity in non-sectarian or intersectarian areas?

8. It occurs to us, too, that we must consider the degree

of religiosity of the metropolitan area and of the particular suburb in which the family lives. Is it accepted practice to attend services, observe *Kashruth* and the Sabbath? How socially advantageous is it to belong to the Synagogue and its institutions? Is there an emphasis on interreligious activities in the community? How does this affect the readiness of the youngster to associate with non-Jews? Does the degree of orthodoxy of the Synagogue or community have more of a bearing in a larger city or less?

9. What is the position of the Jew in the social strata of the city? How do social class and status affect the scope and nature of out-marriage by Jews? Is the Jew a really integrated citizen of the community or is there a reluctance to accept an easily identifiable Jew in the higher echelons of the societal structure? Is there a greater tendency in a large city for some Jews to seek out non-Jewish friends and associates? How does this affect the younger Jew, as he attempts to emulate his businessman or professional parents and older brothers? Does this search for a better class position provide additional motivation toward intermarriage?[7] Is there a difference depending upon the size of the community?

10. Nor should we ignore consideration of the mores of the larger community or the community within the community in relation to intermarriage. Is it easier for an exogamous marriage to be successful in a large city like New York than in a small town? Or does it vary with sections of the city or with other subgroupings within the larger community? Will intermarriage be more acceptable or less pointedly reprehensible in relatively irreverent Greenwich Village than in Hassidic Williamsburgh or even in liberal-humanistic-Yiddishist circles? On the other hand, is intermarriage encouraged in some social, philosophical and/or political circles, thus making it less of a problem for "reluctants" to overcome?[8]

11. To what extent do young Jews accept the "melting pot" philosophy instead of one based upon pluralistic tenets? It would be interesting to know whether educational levels vary in metropolitan areas compared with smaller cities and whether this factor has an effect on the answer to this question.

12. Some studies have evidenced that families which have intermarried, or where collateral branches have done so, show a greater proportion of intermarriage than others. To what extent is this phenomenon more prevalent in the larger city than elsewhere?

13. When we get into the psychological factors in intermarriage,[9] we must be careful not to become so involved in the consideration of these vitally significant components of the problem as to fail to distinguish between the composite interplay of emotional and situational stimuli in Metropolitan Gigantica and the interaction of the same forces in the setting of a town like Smallville. If, for example, we were to agree with the generally accepted concept that an important motivation in intermarriage is often a psychological urge to rebel against one's parents or against the familial situation in which one has been raised, then we might ask ourselves whether the size of the community tends to encourage or to discourage such rebellion in adolescents? Does the urban family differ sufficiently from the rural family to warrant the assumption that city life creates stresses leading to rebellion and, therefore, to a search for emancipation? Is there more emotional disturbance in the big city? Are there other situational elements leading to family difficulties and to resultant dislocations, one of which may be the child's out-marriage?

It might be most enlightening to study in depth a significant number of intermarriages in both large cities and smaller communities, with some emphasis on the various types of sections and of surburban areas of metropolitan areas, to determine what differences do exist in the socio-cultural and psychological milieus of each as they may have some effect upon the incidence of intermarriage between Jews and non-Jews.

It should be added, in conclusion, that the institutional set-up of metropolitan areas offers opportunities for research which have not yet been utilized. We are thinking here of Jewish family and child care agencies, residence halls, Conciliation Boards and the like.

1. Population Statistics—Religion Reported by the Civilian Population of the United States: March 1957—*Current Population Reports*, Series P. 20 No. 79 (February 2, 1958) Table 6.

2. Alvin Chenkin, "Jewish Population in the United States, 1958" (*American Jewish Year Book*, Vol. 60), 9.

3. Alvin Chenkin, "Jewish Population In the United States, 1960" (*American Jewish Year Book* Vol. 62), 53.

4. Fred Massarik, *A Report on the Jewish Population of San Francisco, Marin County and the Peninsula, 1959* (Jewish Welfare Federation of San Francisco) Table 24, 44.

5. Alvin Chenkin, *Op. cit.*, Vol. 60, 8.

6. See Marshall Sklare and Marc Vosk, *The Riverton Study* (American Jewish Committee, 1957), 37.

7. See Maria H. Levinson and Daniel J. Levinson, "Jews Who Intermarry: Sociopsychological Bases of Ethnic Identity and Change" *YIVO Annual of Jewish Social Science*, Vol. 12 (1958-59) 109. They feel that Jewish-Gentile marriage is not primarily a "mobility" phenomenon.

8. See Levinson, *op. cit.*, 120. See also, John E. Mayer, *Jewish-Gentile Courtships* (New York: The Free Press of Glencoe, Inc. 1961) Chapter 10, 179-188.

9. For a psychologically oriented treatment of the subject see Levinson, *op. cit.*

REMARKS ON INTERMARRIAGE IN METROPOLITAN AREAS

By Isaac N. Trainin

As Religious Advisor for the Federation of Jewish Philanthropies of New York and Director of its Commission on Synagogue Relations, I have had the opportunity of working in a community (covering the five boroughs, Westchester and Nassau) which numbers probably over two and a half million Jews.[1] In addition to working very closely with hundreds of rabbis and synagogue leaders, I have also been in a position to cooperate with social workers in a number of Jewish communal agencies, such as family agencies and child care institutions. Let me therefore give you some of the findings, albeit tentative, which have come to my attention from our social work agencies.

Rabbi J. Bemporad, spiritual leader of Hawthorne, a school for emotionally disturbed children, reports that in 1961 approximately 40 per cent of all the children there came from mixed marriages. This was a 10 per cent increase over the 1960 figure. For whatever value one may wish to attach to it, it seems that at Hawthorne there were more girls from mixed marriages than boys. The Jewish

Child Care Association submitted some pertinent figures with the statement that "we have always had an appreciable percentage of children under our care from mixed marriages. However, the number seems to be increasing."

One might be tempted to conclude that perhaps emotionally disturbed children and children who are placed in foster homes because of family breakdowns often come from families in conflict and that, therefore, in such groups the rate of intermarriage might be expected to be higher than elsewhere. Yet, 840 children out of 1093 studied in 1960 by the Jewish Child Care Association came from homes where both parents were Jewish. The implications to be drawn from such figures should be the subject of a separate study.[2]

At Pleasantville, another school for emotionally disturbed children, the most recent statistics indicate that among 178 resident children, 26 were the offspring of mixed marriages. Eleven of the 26 children came from Jewish-Catholic homes, fifteen from Jewish-Protestant homes. It seems that this agency deals with a greater number of females than males who have married outside of their faith. At the Edenwald School for retarded children, out of a client population of 57, there were in 1961 nine children from mixed marriages.

These are only random statistics, but they may be straws in the wind.

Insofar as the intermarriage rate is concerned, we know that the European picture is a bleak one. In some countries the rate of out-marriage among Jews is as high as 50 or 60 per cent of the Jewish marriages.[3] It has also been said that an overwhelming number of American Jewish families of the eighteenth and nineteenth centuries have very few descendants alive today who are Jews. For instance, among the lineal descendants of Haim Salomon, the great American revolutionary patriot, there are today a Protestant Minister and a former United States Ambassador to France, but no Jews. I do not know whether it is true that 20 or 30 per cent, or, as some say, over 90 per cent, of the eighteenth and early nineteenth century American Jewish families are represented in our century by descendants who are Christians. I do know that some of the finest American families today stem from outstanding Jewish families of eighteenth and nineteenth century America. Some of these destroyed their family records so that no one will ever detect that their forebears were Jews, but as to others the records are readily available.[4] In discussing this problem with rabbis and synagogue leaders over a period of ten years and at numerous seminars, one is definitely led to believe that the rate of out-marriage among Jews is on the rise in the New York area. One would like to feel that the frequency of such marriages among non-observant families is higher than among observant ones. Yet, in the last half year, I have personally observed several cases of intermarriage, in all of which the Jewish partners were young men of traditional families who had attended Jewish day schools.

Intermarriage has been a problem at all times for the Jewish people. What amazes me is that in all of America, where Jewish communities spend so much money to maintain an infinite variety of communal institutions, no serious study of out-marriage among Jews has as yet been undertaken. In New York City, the last study made was done in 1918 by Julius Drachsler.[5] We may not be able to do much about people who are determined to out-marry, but we certainly should know the figures, if we are to consider doing anything at all.

It has been said that the rate of out-marriage among Jews in America is not higher than 10 to 15 per cent. If this figure were correct, I would not be disturbed about it. I firmly believe, on the basis of reports from many parts of the country, and especially from small cities, that these figures are way off. Yet, it has been said recently that inter- marriage among Jews in big cities is more frequent than in small communities, which seems to make sense. As a friend of mine from a small community told me only recently, "You know, Rabbi, I come from a small community. If a Jewish boy dates a Gentile, most Jewish families will have nothing to do with him. So some of us boys have to be very careful." In other words, there seems to be a great deal of social control in small communities where people know each other. In a big city, the situation is different. You can live on the same block for 30 years and not know the people on your block at all. You can live in the same apartment for a very long time and have a nodding ac- quaintance with your next-door neighbor, but this is as far as you go. This, of course, prevents strong social ties from arising and makes social control difficult.

I have visited many sections of the New York metropoli- tan area and am amazed at the number of intermarriages in these suburban communities. Recently I attended an engagement party in a town in Westchester County, which is adjacent to the city of New York. The father of the pros- pective bride is a very well-to-do Jew. He is a Jew by birth only who maintains his Jewishness through philanthropy. He belongs to an all-Jewish Country Club. At this engage- ment party I met over forty young couples—friends of the prospective bride. An overwhelming number of them rep- resented mixed marriages. The girl in question was going to marry a Jewish boy whom she happened to have met in the home of a friend of hers, a Jewish girl married to a Catholic man. One wonders what is more important here, the exception or the rule.

I have found similar situations elsewhere in the New York area. Recently, I heard a story about a rabbi in a nearby community who lost his position after only six months in office because he delivered a strong sermon against intermarriage. Yet, how was he to know that several members of his Board of Directors had themselves Christian wives? Let me emphasize that I am referring to couples who have maintained their different faiths in marriage. In a recent pilot study, one of our affiliated agencies found that 36 persons in a caseload of 500 clients lived in intermarriage. These 36 cases came to light during meetings with social workers. Obviously, they do not account for numerous other intermarriages in this caseload because it is not the policy of social work agencies to ask people whether they are intermarried or not. We know further that in large cities a considerable percentage of Jewish people go with their problems to non-sectarian family agencies and not to Jewish-sponsored agencies. Shall we assume that many of these Jews prefer a non-sectarian agency because they do not wish to be identified as Jews and/or because they are intermarried?

Now, what is the over-all percentage of Jewish-Gentile intermarriages in New York? Somebody has claimed that it may be as high as 25 per cent. If it were so, it would be something to be disturbed about. I emphasize that I do not know the facts, and neither does anyone else. I do hope that one of these days somebody wakes up and proposes that every Federation and Welfare Fund in this country, as well as the principal synagogue groups, get together and convene a national conference in order to discuss this problem and raise funds for such a study. It is, however, not enough to talk about a study, one must plan it in all earnest.

Tradition has it that only one-fifth of the Jews left Egypt—four-fifths having been assimilated. Only the good Lord knows how many of our people were lost through assimilation and intermarriage in the past 2,000 years. I know, however, that the future belongs to those who care. If intermarriage is indeed a problem, and, as I suspect, a growing one, then let us get all the facts and figures and interpretations we can possibly lay our hands on. Ways and means may then be found to arrest the trend.

1. C. Morris Horowitz and Lawrence J. Kaplan, *The Jewish Population of the New York Area 1900-1975* (Federation of Jewish Philanthropies of New York, 1959), 17.

2. The argument based on these data cuts both ways. The data would seem to indicate a high incidence of intermarriage among the clients of Jewish social agencies, but they also show that many of the intermarried seek the shelter which these agencies provide. (Editor's Note.)

3. Cf. Prof. Goldberg's paper in this volume.

4. Malcom H. Stern, *Americans of Jewish Descent* (Cincinnati, 1961).

5. Julius Drachsler, *Democracy and Assimilation* (New York, 1920).

CONCLUSIONS

INTERMARRIAGE AGAINST THE
BACKGROUND OF AMERICAN DEMOCRACY

by Werner J. Cahnman

I.

If we want to know what we can do, or not do, about intermarriage, we must try to gain an understanding of what intermarriage is like and under what conditions it takes place. A diagnosis has been presented in the preceding papers from the point of view of the demographer, the sociologist, the psychiatrist, the rabbi, the educator—but the data are incomplete and whatever conclusions may be based on them must remain tentative. However, if we raise our sights beyond the issues of the day and analyze intermarriage in a wider historical context, we may gain a vantage point from which to view the problems of intermarriage in a democracy, even if specific data are lacking.

The record of history shows that wherever two populations have lived side by side in one territory, contacts between them resulted in intermixture or intermarriage to a lesser or larger degree. To start with, when the tribes of Israel entered the land of Canaan and throughout the pe-

riod of the judges and the Kings, such intermingling occurred and when the exiles returned from Babylon it occurred again. The Chinese people would not have grown
to the 700 million multitude they are today, if they had
not absorbed innumerable lesser ethnic units and made
them Chinese. Similarly, in the time of the great migrations
in Europe, roving Germanic tribes were absorbed among
Celto-Roman populations in Italy, Spain and France. Anglo-
Saxons and Normans mixed with Celts in Britain; Finns
and Tatars with Slavs in Russia; Semitic and Hamitic mi-
grants with Negroid peoples in the Sudan; Negro slaves and
soldiers with Arab and Berber populations in the Arabian
Peninsula and in North Africa. One might also remember
the saying that God created the white man and the black
man, but that the Portuguese created the mulatto. The examples can be muliplied. One of the oldest sociological
theories, already known to the ancient philosophers, mas-
terly expounded in the fourteenth century by the great
Moslem scholar Ibn Khaldoun, and reformulated in recent
decades by Ludwig Gumplowicz and Franz Oppenheimer,
states that conquest results in the superimposition of a ruling group over subjected populations and that such original
stratification is followed by amalgamation and the formation of nations. However, peaceful confederations of tribes,
resulting in intermarriage, may have been just as frequent.

In modern mass migration, individuals rather than
groups have met with others of different derivation and
from these contacts ensued first competition, even conflict,
but finally accommodation and assimilation; and "the final
test of assimilation" is intermarriage. This is the "race relations cycle"—rather a race relations sequence—as stated
by Prof. Robert E. Park in Chicago.[1] A foremost example
of such a cycle may be observed in Hawaii. There are other
cycle theories, each describing a somewhat different ideal-
typical sequence of interrelations, but, if there is neither

expulsion or genocide, ultimate fusion, even if long delayed, would seem inevitable. It must be emphasized, however, that what is meant here is physical fusion, not necessarily the blurring of cultural identity. The interpenetration of cultures is no less real than the merger of families, but the process is much more complex. In a way, what I am trying to show in this paper is that cultural or sub-cultural identity can be maintained while physical separateness is not a likely expectation.

Advisedly, we speak of intermixture *and* intermarriage because, even where intermarriage is prohibited or frowned upon, intermixture cannot be avoided. The American Negro provides an example. Regarding specifics, status differentials are decisive. Where there is no equality of status between two groups, there is a) either no intermarriage, only intermixture, with children frequently, but not always, going to the lower caste, or b) intermarriage, but with children predominantly going to the higher status group. In the first instance, the relation is exclusively between males of the superordinated and females of the subordinated group; in the second instance, the preponderance may be either way. In other words, where spouses are of unequal status, extramarital relations are frequent while under conditions of equality of status formal marriage procedures are required at all times. Although in an open class society, such as ours, all forms of liaisons are possible, our concern is chiefly with intermarriage because its formalized character presupposes community sanction.

Contrary to a widely held assumption, the history of the Jewish people after dispersion offers no exception to established rules. The question, here as elsewhere, is, who absorbs whom? When the Jews were in a position of social prestige, they absorbed others, when they were in a position of social degradation—even if they were economically affluent—they were likely to lose to others some of their own. Jews made converts and admitted them into their families in the Roman empire, in North Africa until the advent of Byzantine and Arab rule, and in the early stages of their settlement in Eastern Europe.[2] When their position in the Mediterranean countries deteriorated during the Middle Ages, many became converts to Christianity and Islam. The Marranos of Spain and Portugal are the foremost, but not the only, example. It has been observed that losses to Judaism through intermarriage are likely to mount in times of equality and prosperity, but losses through conversion and desertion are as great, if not greater, in times of distress.[3] Any implication that Judaism should fear freedom and equality is therefore beside the point.

The emancipation in Europe changed the situation insofar as the admission of Jews as citizens implied the abolition of a great many "fences around the Torah" and increased social contact. As a result, intermarriage became a problem, first for the upper strata of Jewish society and then on a broad front. However, the low social prestige—occasional high economic position notwithstanding—in which the Jews continued to be held can be read from the fact that the Jewish partner in the liaison used to be a female and that the children, as a rule, were raised outside the Jewish faith. Nobody fits the pattern better than the famed Rothschilds, who felt obliged to remain observant Jews in the male line while marrying off the females of the species (if no Rothschild cousin was available) to the European aristocracy. Only in recent decades has the scale been tipped in favor of Jewish males marrying non-Jewish spouses, indicating an approach to social equality.[4] The approach was hesitant, though, as may be gauged from the observation that offspring were overwhelmingly lost to the Jewish faith and the Jewish people.

II.

America, heir to European liberalism, never encountered the formal problems of emancipation. It started from the assumption of social and political equality. The task of America was to create a new nation out of the *disjecta membra* of European immigrations, with equal opportunity for all—and may the devil take the hindmost. The Jew was a welcome ingredient in the amalgam, the atmosphere fluid and permissive, settlement—first of Sephardic Jews, then of central European immigrants—geographically far-flung and numerically insignificant. As a result, intermarriage and loss of offspring out of the faith were frequent. However, the mass immigration of Jews from eastern Europe since the 1880's temporarily halted the process, chiefly because of the dense settlement in self-contained Jewish neighborhoods which was generated by that influx.

We know that this period has come to an end, but the indications as to what it has been leading up to are confused. Generally, it is assumed that, with the growing up of a second and third American-born generation, ethnic groups of the "newer" immigration have become integrated into the mainstream of American life, but that intermixture has tended to proceed along religious lines, so that a "triple melting pot" of Protestants, Catholics, Jews, respectively, has come into existence, fusing *"landsmanshaften"* into larger, religiously defined blocks. This is the situation which Ruby Kennedy has described for New Haven.[5] However, the implication that Protestant and Catholic "ethnics" have intermarried among each other as well as with old-stock Americans while the Jews have remained a "residual" group, marrying almost exclusively among themselves, is erroneous. The process of ethnic intermarriage among Jews has never been described, but we know that in the older immigration Sephardic, German-Bohemian and eastern European families have merged and that in the new immigration three numerically unequal groups of new-Sephardic, central European and eastern European Jews have come into existence who in themselves consist of mixed locality groups and whose lines of demarcation against each other begin to appear frayed. In my own family, which is of South-German stock, I have Jewish relatives of French, Italian, Hungarian, Galician and Latvian derivation, in addition to German ones, not to mention Gentiles. Intellectually, perhaps the predominant element in American Jewish life is Lithuanian, with Polish and German ingredients following closely in order of importance, but statistically the picture is entirely blurred. Whatever the mixture, the outcome is bound to be distinctly American.

The point which concerns us here is whether this process of consolidation represents a successful attempt at "self-segregation" or whether the social mobility prevailing in an open class society will break down existing barriers and corrode Jewish life altogether.[6] We can only clarify the question, not provide the answer. First and foremost, both the term and the fact of "self-segregation" would seem to be dubious. Congregation, meaning voluntary association with one's own kind, must be distinguished from segregation, meaning legally and socially enforced separation of one group from another. Consequently, "self-segregation" appears as a mixed term, if not a logical contradiction. Actually, segregation (without the "self") is as much a reality in American life as is voluntary association with one's own kind. This is especially true as far as residential segregation is concerned. For the Chicago area, which is the best documented, the data, as referred to by Erich Rosenthal, point to a considerable amount of discrimination in rental housing as well as in the real estate market, but the extent to which "segregation" of this kind has been instru-

mental in facilitating "congregation" remains unknown.[7]
Also, one must discern between the desire of some Jews to
live near Jewish institutions, especially synagogues, but not
necessarily in separation from non-Jewish neighbors, and
the desire of others to live in communities which are overwhelmingly Jewish in composition. We have data from
New Orleans and Trenton, indicating that there may be
regional differentiations in this regard.[8]

With these reservations in mind, one can nevertheless
agree with Erich Rosenthal that the movement of Jewish
populations from areas of first and second to those of third
settlement frequently has led to new residential concentra-
tions in high-status neighborhoods, not to a wide scatter-
ering over many areas. Congregational tendencies from
within and segregational pressures from without seem to
have coalesced to bring about that result. Perhaps what one
can say is that many American Jews do not strenuously
object to segregational practices in the housing field as long
as they are not prevented thereby from congregating in
high-status neighborhoods, with favorable conditions for
in-group socialization. This is considered a prerequisite for
group survival. Concessions to the general environment are
made in the fields of Jewish education and observance. Apparently, a *modicum* of Jewish content, for instance instruction for the *Bar-Mizwah* celebration, is thought to be necessary, but too much of it is avoided, so as not to jeopardize
cultural integration in America and success in the competitive race. In such a way, "suburbia" symbolizes the desire
to enjoy the best of two worlds.

In an earlier publication, I characterized a large segment
of the Jewish population in metropolitan areas as "culturally American, socially in the Ghetto."[9] Will the fact that
the Ghetto is now "gilded," apart from making it more se-
curely "American," provide a stormproof haven for survival? The available data are not conclusive. In the core

city of San Francisco the intermarriage rate is 17.2%, in the Peninsula 20.0%, in Marin County 37.0%; in the core city of Washington the intermarriage rate is 12.2%, in Montgomery County 11.6%, in Prince George County 20.8% in Virginia 34.2%.[10] It would seem that the high-status suburban counties have a high intermarriage rate, but, then, these are not densely settled Jewish neighborhoods. One would have to wait for intermarriage data from Forest Hills or West Rogers Park as well as from the New York and Chicago suburbs beyond the city boundaries which are largely Jewish before one could make a more definite statement. But if one adds the observation that a high percentage of the younger generations in these newer areas receive a college education and that the intermarriage rate tends to be higher among college graduates than among those who attend only elementary schools or high schools, chances are that the high-status neighborhoods, whether they harbor a considerable percentage of Jews or not, will be a jumping-off ground for accelerated social mobility and a large amount of out-marriage.

It is, of course, trite to say that ours is an associational society. In a caste-like situation, cultural subgroups are likely to be preserved and the individual is confined to them as well as sheltered by them. In an open-class situation, where rapid change is the order of the day and "other-orientation" prevails, the individual is cut loose from his community of birth, and since he cannot rely on his own resources, he must choose new associations, as the occasion demands. In these circumstances, the "triple melting-pot" pattern in America, hardly established, may be scrambled all over again. The neat categories of Protestants-Catholics-Jews are likely to emerge badly blurred—not in the sense that these religious categories are going to disappear, but in the sense that membership in them will be no longer exclusively a matter of birth and hallowed custom, but in-

creasingly a matter of choice. The Protestant denominations as well as the Catholic church are in the grip of this
change. In a nationwide study of marriages of members of
the United Lutheran Church of America, Bossard and Boll
found that 20.5% of them had married Roman Catholics,
18.8% non-Church members and 23.7% other Protestants.[11] Concerning Catholics, Father Thomas reports that
between one-fourth and one-third of all valid Catholic marriages are mixed marriages while an additional 15-25% of
all marriages involving Catholics are invalid.[12] These figures tell us little about the ultimate gains and losses of these
churches, but they do provide a glimpse into the complexity of the situation of which churches and church member-
ships are merely a part. Innumerable ideologies and interests, some of them fleeting, are competing for the individual's attention and claiming his allegiance. American Jews
are finding themselves in the midst of the same situation,
only more so. As a statistical minority and a highly mobile
minority, they may be presumed to be more exposed to
contacts, irrespective of where they live, more sensitive to
the value conflicts, the normlessness, the insecurity which
are the attendants of change. In these circumstances, de-
fenses based primarily on social ties, neglecting cultural
bonds, are not likely to be a permanent barrier.

Another deliberation refers to the concept of marginality. According to Everett V. Stonequist who, together with
his teacher Robert E. Park, has worked out the concept,
"the marginal man . . . is one who is poised in psychological uncertainty between two or more social worlds; reflecting in his soul the discords and harmonies, repulsions and
attractions of these worlds";[13] and what Park and Stonequist had in mind was as much a cultural hybrid, like the
emancipated Jew, as a physical hybrid, like the mulatto.
These two were the prototypes, but the detribalized natives
in the Union of South Africa and the children of immigrant

parents in the United States were included. If this is so, the Jew (and the mulatto) have merely anticipated and felt more keenly the anxieties which derive from contradictions in status in a rapidly changing world. In the meantime, the stage has been enlarged to the point where there is hardly anybody who has not been pried loose from his moorings and thrown into new association here and there and everywhere. In the person of President John F. Kennedy—and there are many like him—the American Catholic is now as marginal as the American Jew; and precisely because of the election of President Kennedy the American Protestant begins to partake of the same situation. Federal judges in the South are marginal, as are conscientious ministers of segregated congregations. Likewise marginal are Republican businessmen who serve in a Democratic administration, officers of the armed forces who engage in political controversy, and wives and mothers who are attached to their careers. In view of the pervasiveness of the phenomenon, the American Jew, whose marginality was recognized already a generation ago, is not like to be saved by residential retreatism. The environment of the "gilded Ghetto" helps Jewish boys and girls to meet, but it does not insure the effectiveness of the encounter. In the long run, it will hardly suffice to keep at bay other forces and attractions. However, the desire, which grows in a world of all-encompassing marginality, to associate with those that are like-circumstanced and like-minded, may constitute a centripetal force for Jewishness, if Jewish life and thought have meaning and content.

The situation remains as dubious as it is dynamic. To summarize our deliberations, thus far, one might say that if contact makes for intermixture and intermarriage, mobility is bound to increase the opportunities for contact a thousandfold. Young people meet on the college campus, in the office, in the factory, by the roadside. Even more important, they climb the ladder of professional success and move out of their social class. They are torn between allegiance to childhood memories and alienation from them. If they meet others who have travelled a similar distance, no matter where these companions come from, they will be attracted by them. The companions may be Jews, but they may as well be Gentiles. Possibly, a Jewish boy will gain a sense of freedom from the attachment of a simple Gentile girl, if she affords him the opportunity to escape from the influence of a domineering mother. In addition, Jewish boys may feel oppressed by the expectation of the relentless pressure of the obligations to which they will be subjected in the families of prospective Jewish spouses. The overwhelming majority of my Jewish students at Hunter College, a few years ago, reported that they live in more or less close proximity to their maternal families while they have little contact with relatives on the paternal side. The question arises whether the mother-in-law-centered Jewish family, as we know it today, is indeed an instrument of survival or whether it has become, if not a deterrent to survival, at least an institution of ambivalence, a frustrating experience. However, as no formal studies are available about the role of the mother and the mother-in-law in American Jewish families, we must stop here.

III.

To maintain Judaism in the fluid environment of a democracy requires a new definition of the situation. The dilemma is real. American Jews cannot give up their belief in democracy and the right of individuals to shape their own lives because that would mean denying that they are Americans and that they have a share in the hopes and aspirations which are the essence of America. But they likewise cannot denounce the continuity of Jewish history, that *"emunah,"* or trust, in their destiny as Jews which is the cornerstone of Judaism. There was a time when it seemed that the melting-pot itself meant redemption, but that honeymoon has long passed. The processes of assimilation in America have a way of shattering the sub-cultures of homogeneous groups which enter into it, but, at the same time, they make for continued discrimination against individuals on account of their faded "backgrounds," thus spreading the infection of normlessness. Then, it appeared to some that the idea of "cultural pluralism," defined in a rather static way, could be opposed to the idea of the "melting-pot," but that turns out now to have been a half-way house.[14] Our friend Professor Horace M. Kallen notwithstanding, I cannot see America—whether "America the Idea" or "America the Fact"—permitting the founding fathers' device *"E Pluribus Unum"* to be interpreted in such a way that the *"plures"* in it could be constituted by clearly marked-off ethnic groups, or ancestral communities of any kind, or even huge religious blocks which are left standing forever. Rather, it seems to me that *"E Pluribus Unum"* referred, and continues to refer, on the one hand, to the association of states in a federal union and, on the other, to the right of the individual citizen to associate freely with other citizens for all lawful purposes, including the purpose of religious worship, religiously sponsored education and religiously sponsored charity. "Cultural Pluralism," as interpreted against the background of the American heritage as well as the mobile American reality of our day, refers to the freedom of voluntary association—no more and no less.

But are the Jews of America a voluntary association? Are they not cast in a mold that was prepared for them in ages past? Are they not a "community" which one can leave or enter only with difficulty, an ancestral faith? They would be less than Jews, if they denied all that. These things are part of what Leo Baeck called the "covenant," which is the foundation of Jewish existence, but there is also what he called the "commandment."[15] The "covenant" is contained in "the voice heard on Sinai" and remains "the heritage of the house of Jacob," but the "commandment" is universal, it goes out—through Israel—to all people. Now, in day-by-day Judaism, these concepts have not been thrown away, but they have been interpreted half-heartedly. The "convenant" has been deprived of its spiritual essence and the residuum understood as "peoplehood"—as if it had not been said that Israel should *not* be "like all the peoples" and that they should be a "holy nation." The "commandment," which is meant for everybody, has been whittled down to the pale thought of a Jewish "mission"—a concept which nobody takes seriously because its chief purpose seems to be to sustain the delusion that one can remain shut up tight and clannish and be an example for all humanity at the same time. I would say that the narrow concept of "peoplehood" and the pale concept of "mission" are neither true to what Judaism stands for nor are they viable in a climate of democracy. If the concept of "peoplehood" should ring genuinely Jewish, it must have a content and if the concept of "mission" should be meaningful, there must be an urge to excel in deeds and to accept fellows— an urge to influence and to missionize.

In the market-place of democracy, the principle of competition rules supreme. The growth of the welfare state has not essentially altered that principle, it has merely given hitherto underprivileged segments of the population a chance to catch up and join in the competitive race. In a mobile, competitive society, there are no fenced-off places, except those harboring petrified remnants somewhere in a forgotten corner; no my-home-is-my-castle attitude can long endure. The homes of a democracy have open porches looking out on Main Street; they are part and parcel of the city's life. In these circumstances, parents cannot prevent their children from leaving old associations for new, if this is what their children want. If the world which Jewish parents represent does not appear attractive to younger generations, parents have no right to say: "Stay with us, be old with us!" Ancient thought and ancient rites retain their value to which we like to return, if the call is compelling enough, but adaptations change. In other words, Jewish youth must not be expected to chain themselves to patterns of adaptations which have outlived their usefulness; rather, Judaism must be rejuvenated. This deliberation has much to do with the manner in which the problem of intermarriage is met. If in a competitive, democratic society, losses are sustained through indifference, intermarriage, even conversion, there is nothing that hinders a confident Jewish community from going out and seeking recruits for its cause. It ill behooves Jews to protest against a program of Christian mission among Jews. Without such a mission, no Christian church would be true to itself and a democratic environment, far from being a deterrent, virtually encourages them to persist in their course. It encourages Jews to do likewise!

Some of the timid guardians of the gates say that this cannot be done because "Judaism is not a missionizing religion," but the historical record does not bear them out. To be sure, the rabbis counselled against conversion either when it came by force rather than conviction, as in the case of the Idumaeans, or in precarious situations, as immediately after the return from the first exile or in the period of the Roman persecutions, when infiltration was feared, or under the rule of the victorious Church, when toleration had to be bought by submission. When apprehension of severe punishment hung over Jewish communities, admission into the community was discouraged, as a principle of caution. But when Judaism was confident, the conversion

of non-Jews was eagerly sought. Queen Helena of Adia-
bene, the King of the Khazars, Count Bodo in the Carolin-
gian empire, and many others of lesser rank were pride-
fully admitted. According to Judah Halevi's celebrated
"Kusari," which deals with the conversion of the King of
the Khazars, conditions of "self-sacrifice, purity, knowledge,
circumcision and numerous ceremonies" were imposed
rather than to accept a mere "theoretical" agreement with
principles accepted, but if the conditions were fulfilled, the
convert was welcome.[16]

Now, if the Judaism of ages past was open to those who
wanted to share the glories and humiliations of Israel, all
the more must the concept of "peoplehood" in a democracy
be kept free of racist implications. A people is not a racially pure strain, nor is it an inbred clan or local group, re-
stricted in numbers and influence and incapable of growth.
Rather, it is defined by common heritage, common interests, common hopes. It is open to all comers who can learn
about heritage, identify themselves with interests, share
hopes. Least of all, are the Jewish people racially pure although this was believed to be true until recently. On an
Armenoid and Mediterranean basis, the Jews contain Nor-
dic, Alpine and Dinaric strains and even Mongoloid, Negroid and other ingredients.[17] Their locality groups, for
instance those in Galicia or in Morocco, are as different as
the general populations in these localities. It is the merit of
Zionism to have brought together the locality groups and
the strains which are contained in them and to have fash-
ioned them into a nation in the state of Israel. In America,
the process is generally known to have led to the formation
of "ethnic" groups. Where the immigrants were merely
villagers from Calabria and Sicily, their children have become Italian-Americans. In the case of the Jews, as C. Bezalel Sherman has shown, the coming together of many locality groups has led to intermingling and the growth of

common institutions;[18] but a further educational effort is needed. The task has two aspects. The segmental groupings must be made conscious of a common "peoplehood" —this process is well on its way—and Judaism must be made equal to other creeds and persuasions, so that those who feel attracted by its lucid rationality and its humanitarian ethos may join it freely and be welcome when they enter.

This has a bearing on the problem of intermarriage. The stronger the cultural consciousness of members of a subgroup within a larger society, the more will they be capable of assimilating into themselves influences which they encounter, rather than be assimilated by them. And if their convictions are strong, marrying out of the faith will be no problem for them. A Martin Buber and a Horace M. Kallen were not afraid that their non-Jewish spouses might deflect them from their course. Another leader in modern Judaism, Mordecai M. Kaplan, had already posed the problem clearly in the 1930's:

... Jews must be prepared to reckon frankly and intelligently with intermarriage as a growing tendency which, if left uncontrolled, is bound to prove Judaism's undoing. They must realize that the power and vitality of a civilization are put to the test whenever the members of different civilizations come into social contact with each other. When that contact results in intermarriage and children are born, the more vigorous civilization will be the one to which the children will belong. For Judaism to accept intermarriage between Jews and Gentiles as legitimate from its standpoint, it must be infinitely more sure of itself than it is at present. What else could urge it on to a revision of its values and a reconstruction of its outlook and mode of life as much as the fact that it must be fully qualified to hold its own against competing civilizations? It must be able to imbue the Jewish partner to a mixed marriage with the willingness to maintain a Jewish home. Since this is the case, Judaism should meet all situations that might lead to mixed marriages not fearfully or grudgingly, but in the spirit of encountering an expected development. With such an attitude toward intermarriage, Judaism would avert the tragedy of Jewish parents who consider the child married to a Gentile as lost to them. With a belief in the integrity and value of his own civilization the Jewish partner to the marriage could achieve moral ascendency, and make Judaism the civilization of the home.

It is only an openly avowed policy of this kind that can make the position of the Jews tenable in America. For nothing is so contrary to the ideal of cultural and spiritual cooperation as the unqualified refusal of one element of the population to intermarry with any other. America should be open to the various cultures within her domains. But she is certain to look with disfavor upon any culture which seeks to maintain itself by decrying the intermarriage of its adherents with those of another culture. By accepting a policy which does not decry marriages of Jews with Gentiles, provided the homes they establish are Jewish and their children are given a Jewish upbringing, the charge of exclusiveness and tribalism falls to the ground. With such an attitude, there would no longer be any occasion for pointing to the racial pride of the Jews. What is valuable is the Jewish social heritage, or civilization, and not physical descent.[19]

Mordecai M. Kaplan's words express the philosophy of democratic Judaism.

IV.

Three sub-problems which are in the nature of application rather than theory ought to be mentioned in the context of our discussion. One is Halakhic in nature and concerns the religious definition of who is a Jew. The other concerns the social position of Jewish girls in the circumstances just described. The third, with religious as well as social implications, is the problem of race relations.

1) The Halakhic problem is up to the rabbinate. There is no justification for clinging to the definition of a Jew as the offspring of a Jewish mother, but not of a Jewish father. To be sure, the *"Torah"* cannot be changed, but it can be interpreted according to time, place and circumstances. If circumstances once required to decide that the child of a Jewish mother should not be excluded from the Jewish community even when it was known or suspected that the father was not a Jew, so circumstances now require to find Halakhic justification for the decision that a child of a mixed marriage may be considered a Jew, if parents, guardians or, after legal maturity, the person in question so desire. A decision of this kind will ease many a vexing marital and educational situation without requiring formal conversion of the non-Jewish spouse.

2) Concerning Jewish girls, the question which arises is the following: What is to become of them, if a considerable number of Jewish boys prefer Gentile girls? Should they play a game of musical chairs and resort to non-Jewish partners? Should they try to convince their Gentile husbands that the children ought to be educated in the Jewish faith, which is Halakhically permissible? But the more incisive answer is that they shall compete more effectively. Reports which I have received from college campuses over the years indicate that Jewish mothers sensitize their daughters more to their rights than to their obligations, so that they insist that their future husbands be conveniently docile in the home, inordinately "ambitious" in the marketplace and capable of satisfying the highest material expectations of "happiness." At this point, a vast new area opens

for systematic study. Are there basic Jewish personality types? What is their adaptive strength and inherent weakness? How do family structure and Jewish-Gentile relations interact? How does family structure affect intermarriage? How are changes being induced? These questions must be asked more searchingly.

3) American Jews would not be sufficiently acculturated Americans, if they were not confronted with a problem of race relations in connection with the problems of intermixture and intermarriage. The specific problem does not primarily arise with regard to the integration into Jewish life of the small colored Jewish communities, especially in New York, although this task should not be neglected. The problem arises in the field of adoption. Although, according to present practice in the State of New York, the religious affiliations of the adopted child and the adopting family should be identical, this principle is thrown overboard when the child is born out of wedlock of a Jewish mother and a colored father. According to Jewish religious law, such a child is considered Jewish. However, in the course of six years (1954-59), the Louise Wise Services, a Jewish child care agency, was compelled to give away more than 150 such children to non-Jewish (Negro) homes because no Jewish families could be found who would have been ready to receive them.[20] Nor are racially mixed married couples readily accepted into the organized Jewish community, which is one of the reasons why defiance of parental authority on the part of Jewish girls is easily deflected into interracial association. It can be predicted that the magnitude of the problem will grow and that, in the decade of the 60's, there will be several hundred cases of children of racially mixed (Jewish-Negro) parentage in the New York metropolitan area alone. To continue the present practice would be unprecedented historically and unsupportable on democratic grounds. I do not overlook the formidable diffi-

culties which stand in the way of a satisfactory solution. All I say is that between liberalism professed and illiberalism practiced there is a discrepancy which must be resolved.

V.

These are some of the things which one can do about intermixture and intermarriage when they occur. Education, not physical proximity alone, is likely to provide the ounce of prevention. What kind of education shall it be? Although adequate research data are not available, my experience in the J. W. B. Survey and the Brownsville study inclines me to think that the cardinal point is that Judaism and Jewishness must not be made to appear as if they were set apart from American life, from modern thought, from the totality of man's record in history.[21] Otherwise, young people are put before a painful choice and an avoidance complex is created. For instance, Jewish life in America should not be conceived of as "supplementary" to American life, but as part and parcel of it.[22] Similarly, Jewish thought ought not to be considered significant only by and for itself, but its strength should be shown as being manifested in the influence which it exerted on the development of western thought of which it is a constituent part and by which it has been influenced in its turn. In this view, Martin Buber, the existentialist philosopher, is one and the same with Martin Buber, the Biblical and Hassidic scholar, and Marc Chagall is a moving interpreter of Jewish life precisely because he represents the turmoil and the torture and the flights of fancy of contemporary humanity. Their message, while Jewish in content, is universal in appeal. Even the Hebrew language is more than the tongue of a people or a particular country—it is *"leshon hakodesh"* (the holy tongue), that is, a depository of high values and a treasure house for all mankind.

Like all history, Jewish history must forever be rewritten to fit the needs of succeeding generations. For this generation, then, Jewish history cannot be, like the work of Graetz, the history of a people of "thinkers" and "sufferers." It cannot be, like the work of Dubnow, the history of an embattled nationality. It cannot even be, like the work of Salo Baron, a history of Jewish institutions. It must be the history of Judaism and the Jewish people in a world setting. In such a view, medieval Judaism reflects medieval thought and participates in shaping it, the Jews of Spain appear as cultural and economic agents on a vast stage, Zionism as a chapter in the larger story of national liberation. In the same vein, the "Jewish élan," as Sam Welles has called it, must be viewed not as a parochial enterprise, but as a contribution to American civilization.[23] The people who have given to this country the service institution of the mail order house and the welfare unionism of the garment trades and a grandiose philanthropy, not to speak of the example of the worker-soldiers of the state of Israel and the contributions of innumerable individuals to all endeavors of life and art, need not hesitate to present themselves to their own children and grandchildren as well as to the public at large as the co-builders of a new world. In such a world we will all be brothers, but each will speak in his own tongue. Intermarriage will then be taken for granted. It will no more be contemplated with fear and trepidation because to be a Jew will have become a matter of distinction.

1. Robert E. Park, "Our Racial Frontier on the Pacific," Everett C. Hughes et al. (ed.), *The Collected Papers of Robert E. Park*, Vol. I, (Race and Culture, Chicago 1952), 138-151; cf. "Race Relations and Certain Frontiers," op. cit., 117-137.

2. One example for many: Lloyd Cabot Briggs, a fellow of the Peabody Museum of Harvard University, who examined 38 men and 70 women in the Jewish community of Ghardaia in the Algerian Sahara

asserts that "the Kabyle Jews of Ghardaia appear to have been converted to Judaism by missionaries from the East. The missionaries eventually sank out of sight in a sea of converts"—but their cultural imprint remained. Cf. *N.Y.T.*, Dec. 3, 1961. Cf. also Lloyd Cabot Briggs, *Tribes of the Sahara* (Cambridge, Mass., 1960), 90: "Physically the Jews of the Mzab look very much like eastern Berbers ... Careful examination only strengthens this visual impression."

3. Carleton S. Coon, "Have the Jews a Racial Identity?" Isaque Graeber and Steuart Henderson Britt (ed.), *Jews in a Gentile World* (New York, 1942), 28.

4. The break occurred around 1880, as far as Germany is concerned. Cf. W. Hanauer, "Die juedisch-christlichen Mischehen," *Allgemeines Statistisches Archiv*, 17 (1928), 515. However, the contention that the ratio of Jewish male—Gentile female marriages to Gentile male—Jewish female ones tends to increase with a greater degree of anti-Semitic feeling present in a given social situation cannot be sustained. As political anti-Semitism increased after 1880, so did assimilation. As a matter of fact, the two conditioned each other. Cf. John E. Mayer, "Jewish-Gentile Intermarriage Patterns: A Hypothesis," *Sociology and Social Research*, Vol. 45, No. 2 (January 1961), 188-195.

5. Ruby Jo Reeves Kennedy, "Single or Triple Melting Pot? Intermarriage Trends in New Haven, 1870-1940," *American Journal of Sociology*, Vol. XLIX, No. 4, (January 1944), 331-39 and R. J. R. Kennedy, "Single or Triple Melting Pot? Intermarriage Trends in New Haven, 1870-1950," *American Journal of Sociology*, Vol. LVIII, No. 1, (July 1952), 56-59.

6. Erich Rosenthal, "Acculturation without Assimilation? The Jewish Community of Chicago, Illinois," *American Journal of Sociology*, Vol. LXVI, No. 3 (November 1960), 275-88.

7. "Housing Discrimination against Jews," *Rights* (Anti-Defamation League II, New York, January-February 1959), 42.

8. Leonard Reissman, *Profile of A Community—A Sociological Study of the New Orleans Jewish Community*. (The Jewish Federation of New Orleans, 1958), 99; Marshall Sklare and Marc Vosk, *The Riverton Study*. (American Jewish Committee, New York, 1957), 37.

9. Werner J. Cahnman, "The Cultural Consciousness of Jewish Youth," *Jewish Social Studies*, Vol. XIV (1952), 195-208; esp. 205.

10. Fred Massarik, *A Report on the Jewish Population of San Francisco, Marin County and the Peninsula, 1959* (Jewish Welfare Federation of San Francisco, Marin County and the Peninsula, Nov. 1959), 44; Stanley K. Bigman, *The Jewish Population of Greater Washington in 1956* (Jewish Community Council, Washington, D.C., May 1957), 123.

11. James H. S. Bossard and Eleanor Boll, *One Marriage, Two Faiths* (New York, 1957), 56.

12. John L. Thomas, S. J., *The American Catholic Family* (Englewood Cliffs, 1956), 155; Bossard and Boll, op cit., 55.

13. Everett V. Stonequist, *The Marginal Man: A Study in Personality and Culture Conflicts* (New York, 1937), 8.

14. Horace M. Kallen first broached the idea of cultural pluralism in 1915 and summed it up in *Culture and Democracy in the United States* (New York, 1924). But the idea, although widely and favorably discussed, did not stem immigration restriction and other manifestations of "un-hyphenated" Americanism. It must be admitted, however, that this observation does not exhaust the problem and that the diversities persist. At this point, reference is made to Horace M. Kallen's newest book, *Cultural Pluralism and the American Idea. An Essay in Social Philosophy* (Philadelphia, 1956), 56ff.

15. Leo Baeck, *The Essence of Judaism.* (New York, 1948), 66f., 77 et passim.

16. Judah Halevi, *Kusari* (transl. by Hartwig Hirschfeld, New York, 1946), Part I, 69.

17. Carleton S. Coon, *op. cit.*, 20-37 and Melville Jacobs, "Jewish Blood and Culture," Graeber and Britt, op. cit., 38-55.

18. C. Bezalel Sherman, *The Jew Within American Society: A Study in Ethnic Individuality* (Detroit, 1961).

19. Mordecai M. Kaplan, *Judaism as a Civilization; toward a reconstruction of American Jewish life.* (New York, 1934), 418-419.

20. "Religious Rule on Adoption Bars many Couples in State," (N.Y.T., October 11, 1959).

21. Publications derived from the Brownsville Study, apart from Werner J. Cahnman, *op. cit.*, are: "Intercultural Education and Jewish Content," *The Reconstructionist*, Vol. XIV, No. 6 (April 29, 1948), 9-15; "Attitudes of Minority Youth: A Methodological Introduction," *American Sociological Review*, Vol. XIV, No. 4, (August 1949), 543-548; "Suspended Alienation and Apathetic Identification," *Jewish Social Studies*, Vol. XVII, No. 3 (July 1955), 53-59; "The Frustrated Escapist," *The Reconstructionist*, Vol. XXIV, No. 2 (March 7, 1958), 17-20.

22. Oscar I. Janowsky, *The J. W. B. Survey* (New York, 1948) 6; Cf. Werner J. Cahnman, "Principles for Jewish Centers," *The Chicago Jewish Forum*, Vol. 7, No. 1 (Fall 1948), 43-47.

23. Sam Welles, "The Jewish Elan," *Fortune* (February 1960), 134-139.

INTERMARRIAGE AND JEWISH EDUCATION

by Jack J. Cohen

A discussion on intermarriage would not be complete without a re-examination of the processes of Jewish education.

First, a few propositions.

1) Good Jewish education cannot automatically prevent intermarriage, although a poor brand will provide an easy rationalization for the young man or woman who falls in love with a non-Jewish partner and who must think through the pros and cons of intermarriage. A sense of obligation to the Jewish group is more easily dispelled when one's vision of Jewish life is negative.

2) Jewish education should be directed to the humanistic enterprise of cultivating fine human beings out of the soil of the Jewish community and the Jewish heritage. The chief purpose of Jewish education should not be to instill Jewish patriotism as we may call it, although such loyalty, hopefully, will be the natural outcome of effective education.

3) Some intermarriage is inevitable in a free environment. Therefore, although the Jewish community should disap-

prove of intermarriage as a policy, it must not view intermarriage moralistically, as an indication of weakness in
character on the part of the Jewish partner. Intermarriages,
it is true, are sometimes contracted as a means of social
or economic advancement and should be evaluated like
any other marriages founded on such motivations. But a
good number of intermarriages are undoubtedly entered
into between men and women who fall in love and who
have so much in common as to enable them to transcend
cultural differences by a variety of compromises. Then,
too, Jewish parents and the Jewish school are often to
blame for failing to provide young Jews with the motivation to perpetuate Jewish life in their own homes.

4) If and when the non-Jewish partner converts to Judaism, the marriage should not be considered an intermarriage. Too many Jewish families, including many lacking
in cultural and religious depth, still view conversion with
great antipathy, as necessarily an insincere step. This psychology must be overcome in favor of the warm acceptance
of the converted party as a member of the family and the
Jewish community.

The Question of Identity

These propositions suggest a number of implications for
Jewish education.

The first is that the Jewish school must strive to convey
to the Jewish child the nature of his Jewish identity. What
is a Jew? is an underlying question which must receive
constant attention if Jews, in their maturity, are to understand and to accept for themselves the opposition of our
people to intermarriage.

It is necessary that the Jewish school formulate an adequate theory of the morality of Jewish survival. While no
group need morally respond to the challenge of outsiders
to its right to exist, it must raise for itself the query as to

the purpose of its existence. That is to say, every group has the right to perpetuate itself insofar as this constitutes no threat to the survival of other groups. But from a moral standpoint, it has to answer to itself whether or not it is serving a humane function. Thus the Jew need not justify to the anti-Semite his right to exist, but he must ask himself what human purpose he hopes to accomplish as a Jew.

Traditional Judaism had a ready answer to the question of survival. The chosen people doctrine was the source of the Jew's morale. The peculiar relationship between God and Israel determined Israel's career and "justified" its existence. Much nonsense has been written concerning the idea of chosenness, not the least of which is the assertion that chosenness and uniqueness are identical categories. From the standpoint of Jewish education, it is, of course, necessary to define the uniqueness of Jewish historical experience. Chosenness, however, implies a relationship between God and Israel which raises serious theological and social difficulties for persons trained in a spirit of democratic equalitarianism. Nevertheless, for the sake of getting at the root of the educational problem, I am prepared to accept the argument that the doctrine of chosenness can be so interpreted as to render it morally and theologically acceptable.

Jewish education cannot afford to play loosely with the issues that this answer to the question of Jewish survival raises. In the first place, the Jewish school must present the doctrine in its historical and philosophical completeness. It is simply untrue, for example, that chosenness never implied dominion, as any perusal of Isaiah 45:14 and 49:22-23 will testify. Nor is the idea of racialism foreign to various strands of the doctrine, as is manifest in passages in such vastly contrasting documents as Halevi's *Kuzari*[1] and Kohler's *Jewish Theology*.[2] Historically, too, the doctrine was associated with promises concerning the borders of Eretz Yisrael. What is now the status of such promises? Granted that at its best chosenness implies ethical responsibility (cf. Amos 9:2), is this not the equal obligation of every other group? Is *"noblesse oblige"* not an assertion of superiority? If one insists that Jews historically were the first to hear the ethical call, does this historical fact confer upon Jews a status which must be *sui generis* to the end of time? And how does one support theologically the comparative mood of chosenness in the traditional liturgy?

Such concerns aroused by an historical investigation of the chosen people doctrine touch on the moral problem of Jewish survival. All Jewish educators would accept the idea that whether one uses the doctrine or not, the justification for the Jew of Jewish survival must be the desire of the Jewish people to help bring about the Kingdom of God on earth. Such a vocation, if spelled out in the institutions of Jewish life, would be a minimum replacement (or fulfilment) of chosenness in a democratic society.

The responsibility of the Jewish school cannot end with a moral assertion. It must clarify for the student the social context of Jewish life and help him to see operationally what it means to be a Jew in twentieth century America. This is a sociological, as well as a moral and theological matter and entails an analysis both of the American scene (including the religious polities of Catholicism and Protestantism) and of the status of world Jewry. Such a study obviously will depend for its success on the ability of the school to hold the student through the high school years. For an understanding of the subtle distinctions between Judaism and Christianity requires a mature, informed mind. It is just these distinctions which are pertinent in the problem of intermarriage.

This is not the place to answer in detail the question of Jewish status which I have just raised. Enough has been said, however, to indicate that Jewish identity is more likely to be a question of *existential* involvement in the life of the Jewish group than it is one of *essential* acceptance of a set of theological or ethical ideas. It is for this reason that intermarriage is a threat to Jewish survival. If being a Jew merely involved belief in certain ideas of God, Israel, and human behavior, intermarriage might serve as a strengthening force. For it would enable Jews to spread those ideas to other groups. That it does not have the effect of strengthening Jewish life shows that being Jewish embraces many psychic and cultural habits that are lost when the Jewish partner is pulled away from active participation in Jewish life or from loyalty to the Jewish group.

Jewish education can at least help the young American Jew overcome the tendency to approach intermarriage solely from the idealistic but shallow perspective of "love conquers all." To the extent that the school has been able to bring about a sense of Jewish identity which is more than the moralistic "I don't deny I'm a Jew" and which, on the contrary, is profoundly expressed in a way of life, it will have confronted the Jewish student with a number of psychological considerations which he will find it difficult to avoid in the case of an impending intermarriage.

A Moral Case

I have underplayed the moral aspects of intermarriage, because I do not see how any group in a free society can readily adopt a moralistic attitude toward such crossings of the lines. Freedom implies the moral right of every individual to seek his happiness wherever he can find it.

However, one of the functions of Jewish education is to show the Jewish child how the pursuit of happiness can be conducted within the Jewish group and by means of the Jewish tradition. Admittedly, such an endeavor seeks to bind the student to the Jewish people and to discourage his seeking elsewhere for an outlet for his personal development.

The previous two paragraphs are not contradictory in the life situation, but they do point to the responsibility of the Jewish school to spell out for the child the extent to which loyalty to the Jewish people is a moral demand on the Jew. Loyalty in the form of blind patriotism or loyalty based on irrational, racist doctrines is, of course, to be eschewed. But the school is obligated to demonstrate to the child the nature of the forces bent on destroying Judaism and the Jewish people, and to help him assess the moral implications of the defections from Jewish ranks resulting from intermarriage. The school should convey to the child some sense of *kiddush hashem* (sanctification of the Name), of the long centuries of self-sacrifice and devotion that enabled the Jewish people to survive in adversity. And not only to survive, but to maintain a moral and spiritual level to which many modern peoples have not yet attained.

The burden of proof rests on the Jew who would deprive his people of another family to demonstrate that marrying outside the fold will strengthen the forces of goodwill in the world. Beleaguered Jewry cannot afford to release its members from this degree of moral concern about the consequences of intermarriage.

It follows that Jewish education should revise the traditional attitude toward conversion for the purpose of marriage. Traditionally, Judaism has been opposed to accepting converts whose main rationale for becoming Jews is marriage. The arguments in favor of this stringency are clear and well founded—the sincerity of the convert is questionable, hypocrisy is encouraged, easy conversion leads others to look for mates outside the Jewish community, the Jewish home loses some of its depth, and the like. Yet these objections for all their cogency, must henceforth be viewed as precautions to the rabbis in charge of the process of conversion, rather than as deterrents to conversion itself.

The reason for this suggested change in approach is that a pose of isolationism in an environment of freedom will surely weaken the case for Judaism. If the social mobility of democratic society inevitably brings Jews into closer touch with non-Jews, the Jewish group cannot successfully defend itself by preaching isolation. The marriage mart has become an arena of competition, within which American religious sub-groups must struggle for the loyalty of their adherents. Such competition, if conducted fairly and in a spirit of mutual good-will, can have a salutary effect on the spiritual and ethical quality of all American religions, for it will challenge each religious group to live up to its highest potentialities. Under such competition, American Jewry cannot afford to rule out the possibility that many fine young men and women can be induced to opt for Judaism in the event of intermarriage.

The High School

The foregoing analysis will lead to constructive results only if the secondary and college levels of Jewish education do their job. It is idle to expect that the suggestions concerning Jewish identity and the moral challenge of intermarriage are completely communicable to pre-*Bar Mitzvah* students or that the predispositions planted in the elementary years can carry over, without intervening reinforcement, into the pre-marital stage of life.

It is a startling fact, revealed in the recent survey of Jewish education conducted by the American Association for Jewish Education, that less than 8 per cent of those students who receive any kind of Jewish education continue their studies in the high school years. And those who complete the high school studies have been estimated as no more than about 2 per cent.[3] These figures raise a number of interesting questions.

In the first place, the relative infrequency with which Jews out-marry, as compared with Protestants and Catholics, suggests that there are factors in Jewish life which act as a brake, factors which appear to be stronger than the prevailing ignorance of Judaism on the part of Jews. If and when the Jewish school reaches a larger number of adolescents, it would be aided in its work by knowledge of these influences. Indeed, it can hardly be expected to function without an awareness of them. Even without an accurate, scientific diagnosis, therefore, the Jewish high school course can begin to explore with its students the meaning of anti-Semitism, the nature of Christianity, the uniqueness of Judaism, the psychology of filial piety, and the other possibilities that suggest themselves as explanations of the hold which Judaism has even on uninformed Jews.

Secondly, the low figures of secondary school attendance suggest that the high school has thus far failed to give the impression that its course of study is relevant to the needs of the overwhelming majority of American Jewish youth. I say *impression,* because there is undoubtedly much subject matter in current curricula which would benefit the average Jewish boy or girl. But by and large, the Hebrew high school has clearly failed to relate itself to the intellectual and social environment of American Jewish life and particularly to the overriding problem of Jewish survival in a free, but Christian culture.

A question like the ethics of survival in a democratic society should be used by our educators to exercise the minds and hearts of our adolescents and to point up to them the profound issues toward which Jewish life is directed. While no sure-fire guarantee against intermarriage can be supplied, a high school curriculum which deals with the important life questions of our youth can certainly reinforce the other deterrents to intermarriage that operate among Jews. Needless to add, I am not here recommending that the high school program be compounded of current questions to the exclusion of classic texts and the historical tradition. Clearly, the treatment of many contemporary issues can arise out of an examination of the hallowed texts of study.

Thirdly, the figures further suggest that only a small percentage of Jewish youth have a chance to air their questions about interreligious dating and marriage under the guidance of competent counselors. Even assuming that many more Jewish youth are enrolled in clubs and youth movements than attend formal classes, neither they nor their leaders possess the kind of grounding in Jewish tradition which would enable their discussions of intermarriage to rise above the moralistic level. Considering also the fact that the curricula of our Hebrew high schools rarely encourage the students to articulate their life concerns, we come up with the picture of an ostrich-like approach to intermarriage. American Jewry buries its head, hoping that somehow or other the problem will disappear.

The College Level

The last chance American Jewry has to educate against intermarriage (or at least to encourage the establishment of a Jewish home by the conversion of the non-Jewish mate) occurs in college. Here the picture is even blacker than on the secondary level.

The most devastating aspect of the college situation is the Jewish college instructor. Generally a brilliant student and often a fine, idealistic teacher, the Jewish academician is all too frequently a cynical Jew. Often, he himself has out-married. The instructor's marital status, moreover, reflects a general attitude of the Jewish college teacher toward Jewish life. He most often lacks even a sound elementary education in Judaism and sees no reason why he should acquire one. His intellectual concerns are largely confined to his area of competence, and Judaism, at best, is a subject matter in which he has no reason to delve. The example of such a teacher, who is respected on the campus, speaks louder than words to the impressionable Jewish youth.

Of course, the situation is not all one-sided. Every campus has its Jewish staff members who are devoted Jews, and Hillel directors can usually count on a few men and women who will be helpful to their programs. But certainly, even on campuses where there are a large number of Jewish instructors, the impression given by the Jewish teachers is one of apathy. The effect on the morale of Jewish students is devastating.

Secondly, the intellectual aura of the campus emanates from a profoundly Christian origin, often unconscious. The history of Western culture is so overladen with Christian assumptions, that it will take generations of objective study before even the most competent student can distill the mythic elements out of the supposedly factual account of the making of the modern mind. In such a surrounding, the Jewish student can hardly be expected to substantiate intellectually the claims of Jewish individuality and of Jewish survival. Add to this the pressure of a surface liberalism among collegians which would wipe out all ethnic distinctions (in favor, of course, of an unarticulated, but distinctive "Americanism" or "cosmopolitanism"), and the Jewish student is almost totally disarmed.

Thirdly, the Jewish college student must finally face the challenge of free social intercourse. Released from parental supervision and encouraged by the experimental socialization toward which many young Catholics, Protestants and Jews alike reach out, the Jewish student is challenged by the attraction of non-Jewish "dates." And indeed, why not? Can anyone legitimately—that is, morally—argue against such dating? To attempt to apply moral strictures is to raise the hackles of resistance and, indeed, to seek to restore a social ghetto. Furthermore, to discourage dating on the ground that it can lead to marriage presupposes that the student himself opposes such an eventuality. It is this very question which the student has to be helped to argue through for himself. In brief, the college situation removes the last thread of the cocoon which has protected the young Jew from thorough contact with his non-Jewish peers.

It can, of course, be argued that what Jewish education has failed to do until this point, it cannot accomplish in the brief moments available during college. Surely, however, this is a pessimistic view. For there are other aspects to the college scene which Jewish educators cannot afford to disregard.

In the first place, the young Jew is no fool. He may have a warped Jewish education or none at all; he may have universalist visions of society, he may want to find acceptance in the majority culture; and he may look with contempt upon the hypocrisy of his parents and the shallowness of their Jewish way of life. But he is alert, and he tries to be honest. He is, therefore, open to cogent argument, to fact, and to sincerity. He can be reached through books and through sound scholarship, and he is often able to weigh the evidence of creative Jewish survival against the negative evaluations or indifference of his instructors. The very existence of the Jewish people and its cultural alertness give the lie to the distorted role accorded it by Western scholarship. Many a Jewish student has found his way back to Judaism through the sheer weight of his reasoning power.

Nor is the Jewish college student blind to the nature of the marriage bond. Intellectually, at least, he knows that the American romantic conception of love is inadequate to the real complexity of the relationship. He understands or is at least aware of the roles of culture and religion in marriage and he is rarely permitted by his own family to underestimate the influence of family ties. Having learned something of the dynamics of social change, he is likely to acquire a more sympathetic insight into the difficulties of Jewish adjustment to the environment. Such insight has, at times, drawn young people closer to their parents.

Against this background is cast the work of the Hillel Foundations. The poor Hillel director is expected to be the campus representative of the family, charged with preventing any interreligious entanglements that might lead to marriage, to stimulate and to satisfy an appetite for Jewish study that had previously been dormant, and to fight the intellectual battle of Judaism against all comers—manifestly an impossible task. The Hillel director, however, would have to be invented, if he did not already exist, and he must be helped by the Jewish community to fulfil his educational responsibility. Instead of adopting a critical pose toward the work of Hillel, pulpit rabbis, for instance, ought to make it their business to maintain a closer personal contact with their congregants at college. They should encourage their youth to participate in Hillel and to be helpful to its director.

Some agency—perhaps *B'nai B'rith* itself—should seek to organize a Jewish counterpart to the University Christian Fellowship, in which Jewish college instructors could find an outlet, on their level, for their concerns with Jewish life or be stimulated to take an interest in Judaism. Somehow or other, the Hillel director must be made to feel part of a campus team, rather than a lone missionary in the midst of a courteous, but antagonistic "heathen" population. The Jewish community must campaign to capture its intellectuals.

Again, the motivation of such activity cannot be the prevention of intermarriage. The emphasis must be solely on the positive aspect, the building of the case for Judaism and its perpetuation.

Conclusion

There are no panaceas, educational or otherwise, for the problem of intermarriage. As a matter of fact, its ever-present possibility can and should elicit among Jews a creative response, causing us to look to the quality of our family relationships, our communal enterprises, our cultural concerns. By causing us to raise our sights in all these aspects of living, the threat of intermarriage is the necessary "leaven in the dough." The price of freedom is the tension caused by our desire to survive in the face of inevitable competition. In the long run, then, the answer to intermarriage is the quality of Jewish life, for the enhancement of which Jewish education is the main instrument.

1. Yehuda Halevi, *Kuzari*, Book I, paragraph 27.

2. K. Kohler, *Jewish Theology* (Cincinnati, 1943), pp. 38-39, 326-328, 445-446.

3. *Survey of Jewish Education*, compiled by Alexander E. Dushkin and Uriah Z. Engelman, publ. by the American Association for Jewish Education (New York, 1959).

CONTRIBUTORS

BAAR, JACOB, is the Editor of *The Statistical Bulletin,* Metropolitan Life Insurance Company, New York.

BEN-HORIN, MEIR, is Associate Professor of Education at Dropsie College for Hebrew and Cognate Learning, and Managing Editor of the *Jewish Social Studies.* He is the author of *Max Nordau—Philosopher of Human Solidarity,* and has published essays in a number of scholarly journals. He serves on the Board of Editors of *Judaism,* and as a Contributing Editor of the *Reconstructionist.*

CAHNMAN, WERNER J., is Visiting Associate Professor of Sociology at the Newark College of Arts and Sciences, Rutgers University, an Associate Editor of the *Reconstructionist,* and a member of the Child Guidance Committee of the Federation of Jewish Philanthropies of New York. He taught formerly at Fisk and Atlanta Universities, Brooklyn College, Hunter College and Yeshiva University, and served as Executive Director of the Conference on Jewish Social Studies in New York. He is the author of numerous papers on race and intercultural relations and sociological theory. Professor Cahnman was the organizer of the Conference on *Intermarriage and Jewish Life*.

CHENKIN, ALVIN, is Supervisor, Research and Statistical Unit, Council of Jewish Federations and Welfare Funds in New York.

COHEN, JACK J., formerly Rabbi of the Society for the Advancement of Judaism and a Director of the Jewish Reconstructionist Foundation in New York, is presently a Director of the B'nai B'rith Hillel Foundation at the Hebrew University in Jerusalem and Chairman of the United Synagogue Commission on Jewish Education. He is the author of *The Case for Religious Naturalism* and of numerous papers on Jewish education and the philosophy of Judaism.

EICHHORN, DAVID M., Rabbi, is Director of Field Operations, Commission on Jewish Chaplaincy, National Jewish Welfare Board, New York. He is the author of *Cain: Son of the Serpent* and of numerous magazine articles on the subject of mixed marriage and conversion.

ROSENBERG, LOUIS, is the National Director of the Bureau of Social and Economic Research of the Canadian Jewish Congress in Montreal, Canada, and a member of the Board of Directors of YIVO-Jewish Scientific Institute and of the Advisory Board of the *Jewish Journal of Sociology*. He was formerly Director of the Jewish Colonization Association in Western Canada and of the Western Division of the Canadian Jewish Congress. He is the author of a number of scholarly papers on the demography of the Jews of Canada.

KENNEDY, RUBY JO REEVES, is Professor of Sociology and Chairman of the Department of Sociology and Anthropology at Connecticut College, New London, Conn. She has formerly taught at Texas State College for Women and Vassar College. Her research and published papers have been chiefly in the fields of ethnic and religious intermarriage and mental disorders. Her paper "Single or Triple Melting Pot: Intermarriage Trends in New Haven 1870-1940" is widely quoted.

MAIER, JOSEPH, is Professor of Sociology and Chairman of the Department of Sociology and Anthropology at the Newark College of Arts and Sciences, Rutgers University, Newark, New Jersey. He is the author of *Cooperative Living*, co-author of *Sociology—The Science of Society* and a contributor to Jewish and sociological journals. His main interest is in the sociology of religion.

ROSENTHAL, ERICH, is Associate Professor in the Department of Sociology and Anthropology at Queens College, Flushing, New York. His research and published papers have been chiefly in the field of race and intercultural relations and the demography of the Jews in the United States.

RUBENSTEIN, RICHARD L., Rabbi and psychologist, is Director of the B'nai B'rith Hillel Foundation and Chaplain to Jewish students at the University of Pittsburgh and the Carnegie Institute of Technology in Pittsburgh, Pa. He is Associate Editor of the *Reconstructionist* and author of numerous articles on Jewish and psychological topics.

TRAININ, ISAAC N., Rabbi, is Advisor on Religious Affairs of the Federation of Jewish Philanthropies of New York and Director of its Commission on Synagogue Relations. He was formerly Director of Religious Activities for the United Service for New Americans.

WEISBERGER, RAPHAEL M., worked as Circuit Rabbi for the North Carolina Association of Jewish Men, in which capacity he served a number of small Jewish communities unable to engage Rabbis of their own. He is at present Director of Education at Temple Beth El in Stamford, Connecticut.

ZUKERMAN, JACOB T., social worker and lawyer, is
President of the Workman's Circle and Executive Director and Chief Counsel of the Family Location Service, an agency of the Federation of Jewish Philanthropies of New York.